Pierre Janton

Esperanto

LANGUAGE, LITERATURE, AND COMMUNITY

Edited by HUMPHREY TONKIN

Translated by HUMPHREY TONKIN, JANE EDWARDS, and KAREN JOHNSON-WEINER

STATE UNIVERSITY OF NEW YORK PRESS

Originally published as L'ESPÉRANTO
© Presses Universitaires de France, 1973
Published in Esperanto as HET ESPERANTO
© Esperanto Centrum Nederland, 1987

Published by
State University of New York Press, Albany

© 1993 State University of New York

Printed in the United States of America

For information, address State University of New York
Press, State University Plaza, Albany, N.Y., 12246

Production by E. Moore
Marketing by Theresa A. Swierzowski

Library of Congress Cataloging-in-Publication Data
Janton, Pierre.
    [Esperanto. English]
    Esperanto: language, literature, and community / Pierre Janton;
edited by Humphrey Tonkin; translated by Humphrey Tonkin, Jane
Edwards, and Karen Johnson-Weiner.
        p.   cm.
    Rev. translation of: L'esperanto.
    Includes bibliographical references and index.
    ISBN 0-7914-1253-9 (alk. paper).—ISBN 0-7914-1254-7 (pbk.:
alk. paper)
    1. Esperanto.   I. Tonkin, Humphrey.   II. Title.
PM8208.J313   1993   91-42318
499'.992—dc20   CIP

10 9 8 7 6 5 4 3 2 1

Contents

Editor's Preface

Pierre Janton's survey of Esperanto and the Esperanto movement, *L'espéranto*, was first published in 1973 in the *Que sais-je* series by Presses Universitaires de France. A second edition followed in 1977. Translations into Spanish (1976), German (1978), and Dutch (1987), were also published. In 1988 a completely revised edition of the volume appeared, recast into Esperanto by the author and with considerable additional material. Entitled *Esperanto: Lingvo, literaturo, movado*, it was published in Rotterdam by the Universal Esperanto Association.

Some years ago, aware of the lack of a good introduction to the phenomenon of Esperanto for English-speaking readers, I began work on a translation of Janton's study from the original French, enlisting the help of Jane Edwards and Karen Johnson-Weiner along the way. Our translation, which benefited enormously from the linguistic expertise of Dr. Johnson-Weiner, was substantially complete when Professor Janton delivered the manuscript of his new edition to Rotterdam. Following the publication of that edition, I reworked the text, using the Esperanto version as the basis for the translation, but preserving occasional passages or details from the French where this seemed appropriate and updating information throughout, to take into account developments of the past few years. I also prepared a set of notes, designed particularly to assist the English-speaking reader, and an extensive bibliography, again with the English reader in mind. In the present edition, all notes are mine, except where the initials P. J. indicate that they come from the French or Esperanto originals, and I have also reworked passages on contemporary Esperanto literature and the current Esperanto movement in the chapters concerned with these topics.

I am most grateful to Drs. Edwards and Johnson-Weiner for

their assistance and to Professor Janton for his help at every stage. The need for this translation has long been felt by those of us active in Esperanto studies in English-speaking countries. The book remains the best general introduction, by a specialist in language and literature, to the entire topic of Esperanto and its role in the modern world.

HUMPHREY TONKIN

Abbreviations

Let   *Leteroj*, the letters of Zamenhof, edited by Gaston Waringhien, 2 vols. (Paris: Sennacieca Asocio Tutmonda, 1948).

LPLP   *Language Problems and Language Planning.*

OV   *Originala verkaro*, the collected original works of Lazar Ludwik Zamenhof, edited by J. Dietterle (Leipzig: Ferdinand Hirt, 1929).

Introduction

Esperanto appears simple, but it is a phenomenon of considerable complexity. We can approach it in several different ways.

First, we can see it as one artificial, or planned, language among several hundred such projects, studying it as an example of a consciously created linguistic system. We can examine it either in isolation or in relation to other planned languages (or interlanguages). This comparative approach derives from a special branch of linguistics known as interlinguistics, so named by Jules Meysmans and by the Danish scholar Otto Jespersen around 1930.[1] However, it is not limited to linguistic typology, since its main object of study is a wholly unique phenomenon: the transition from a planned language, created by a single individual, to a modern living language spoken widely in certain international circles. This evolutionary process merits detailed research, not only because the conscious linguistic creation characteristic of planned languages[2] constitutes an original and virtually untouched field of study, but also because in the present stage of Esperanto's development we can observe unconscious impulses operating alongside the conscious ones. In other words, Esperanto is beginning to develop independently, not only through the conscious decisions of its speakers but also in accordance with its own internal rules, as do all living languages (see Wells 1978).

Second, as an ideological phenomenon Esperanto is of interest to the historian of ideas. It was conceived as a solution to the problem of communication caused by multilingualism in the world. This problem rose to prominence in the seventeenth century and has persisted as social, scientific, and technological changes have reinforced the need for wider linguistic communication. Esperanto is no isolated phenomenon in human history, or in Europe, or in its own day. It originally derived from a growing awareness not only of the form of international communication but also of its content. In this sense, a commitment to Esperanto is more than a commitment to a theory of an ideal world language: it implies a theory of the purpose of language, and this implied theory is in turn a form of humanism. The term *Esperantists* is commonly reserved for those users of Esperanto who agree with the humane values behind the language.

Third, Esperanto is a psychosociological phenomenon. This aspect of the language became apparent almost as soon as it was created. A language cannot develop without a growing group of speakers. Thanks to the "Lingvo Internacia," a movement came into being that today extends to over a hundred countries. Although people of many nationalities and social backgrounds work together in this movement, it maintains a fundamental unity of purpose, less because of its formal organization than because of its psychological impetus. Throughout its hundred-year history, the Esperanto movement has attracted and blended various ideologies and political and psychological tendencies, creating out of them a genuine Esperantist consciousness, based on a broad sense of high ideals (Forster 1982; Lapenna, Lins, and Carlevaro 1974).

The preceding remarks give some idea of the cultural and humanistic values of Esperanto. This living language—in fact the only living planned language—derives its strength from the growing number and diversity of its users. And the more the numbers and the diversity increase, the more Esperanto's powers of expression grow and the more clearly its unique characteristics become apparent. As an international language, Esperanto aspires to the role of auxiliary language currently filled by a few imperialistic national languages. Other planned languages, before and after Esperanto, have espoused a similar goal, but have failed. Because of its firm linguistic, ideological, and sociological foundation, Esperanto has already begun to perform this function in many areas of literature and science. Through Esperanto translation, several masterpieces of little-known or minority cultures have gained a worldwide audience and reached levels of society normally indifferent to foreign literatures. Above all, an abundant original literature, comparable with national literatures and sometimes even richer, attests to Esperanto's linguistic and artistic maturity (Auld 1981, 1984; Tonkin and Hoeksema 1982).

Chapter 1

Esperanto and Planned Languages

The history of planned languages really begins in the seventeenth century. The requirements of order, harmony, and purity of style, characteristic of classicism, brought national languages to what seemed their highest perfection. The literatures that blossomed in these languages, while declaring themselves faithful to Greek and Latin models, claimed equal privileges and equal value. While a humanist like Juan Luis Vives could not imagine an international language other than Latin, Comenius (Jan Amos Komenský), a century later, could not imagine Latin continuing to play that role. However, not only the growing awareness of linguistic difference and diversity—the first Quechua grammar appeared in 1560—and not only the declining suitability of Latin, but a fundamental unhappiness with all natural languages led the philosophers of the day to concern themselves with the language problem. They questioned the epistemological value of words as means of thought and cognition, and some even believed that language learning was more damaging than useful because it drew attention to words rather than things. They sought to construct a universal knowledge system, in which words or symbols would have a regular and logical, rather than arbitrary and incoherent, relation to reality. Accordingly, they · analyzed mind in terms of ideas, listing these ideas and their components and assigning a specific symbol to each.[1]

This approach is exemplified in a letter from René Descartes to Marin Mersenne (20 November 1629). Descartes acknowledges that a simplified or refurbished grammatical system that could be learned in five or six hours would be a useful discovery. But in his view the learning of artificial words would be as difficult as learning the words of a national language, unless they could be derived from one another through a logical sequence conforming to the structure of the mind, "that is, by establishing order among all elements of thought in the human mind, just as there exists a natural order among numbers." Much as in a single day we can learn to count to infinity, so we would be able to learn the names of all things. "And if one were to analyze human thought in all its constituent elements, and if everyone agreed with this analysis, I daresay that a universal language, easy to learn, pronounce and write, would follow, and that, more importantly, this language would aid judgment by presenting all things to the individual so clearly that error would be virtually impossible."[2]

There was widespread agreement on the utility of a universal language, but it was also widely believed that it would be useful not only as a means of communication but also as a classifying and clarifying device—in fact as a general tool for finding and testing truth. Two years before his death, Gottfried Leibniz dreamed of a language "in which all reasonable truths would be reduced to a kind of calculation ... and errors, except those of fact, would be nothing more than errors of calculation. It would be very difficult to create or invent this language or character, but extremely easy to learn it without a dictionary. It would also serve to estimate degrees of probability when we lacked sufficient information to arrive at certain truth."[3]

The universal-language projects that appeared in increasing numbers from about 1650 on used as their starting point the Cartesian postulate that "invention of this language depends on true philosophy." Posited on the classification of ideas, they constituted coherent systems ordered around sets of fundamental concepts. Thus the "philosophical language" of the Scotsman George Dalgarno (London, 1661) distinguishes seventeen classes of ideas, each designated by a capital letter, from which all related ideas can be derived through combinations of Greek and Latin letters: N = living being; Nη = animal; NηK = quadruped; NηKa = horse.[4]

The continuity of such languages from the seventeenth to the twentieth centuries is remarkable. In 1795 J. Delormel presented to the French government a project based on the same principles: Ave = letter; Alve = vowel; Avi = syllable; Avau = word; Alvau = name. In 1852, just thirty-five years before Esperanto, a project by Sotos Ochando had a similar structure: A = things; Ab = material objects; Aba = elements; Ababa = oxygen. Such systems developed into mere classifications: it is no surprise that the famous Decimal System of Melvil Dewey produced the project Translingua, in which 7131 was a lion (7 = animals), $^{1}7131$ a lioness, 7131^{2} leonine, and so on.

Thus, as Cartesian theory developed and was put into practice over the centuries, it tended to emphasize classification and to overlook language itself. It was not concerned with what conventions were to be used to distinguish ideas and their relationship to one another: one could equally well choose an alphabetical or a numerical system, or a combination of the two, or indeed any other system. Most projects, however, fit into two categories: pasigraphies and pasilalia.

PASIGRAPHIES

A pasigraphy, or universal character, is a purely visual writing system. Pasigraphies can use letters, numbers, signs, ideograms, hieroglyphics, or even musical notation, as in the case of Jean Sudre's Solresol (1866). They derive from the tradition we have just encountered and are based on the classification of ideas. Pasigraphies flourished until the end of the nineteenth century: for two hundred years linguists believed that pasigraphy would have to form the basis of any universal language.

The word *pasigraphy* appeared for the first time in a treatise by J. de Maimieux entitled *Pasigraphy, or the First Elements of a New Art and Science of Writing and Printing in a Language to Be Read and Heard in All Other Languages without Translation* (Paris,

1797).[5] The whole system was based on twelve fundamental signs which, when combined in threes, fours or fives, formed the entire vocabulary. However, the principle existed long before the term was coined. In 1668 the English bishop John Wilkins published *A Real Character and a Philosophical Language*, in which he distinguished forty classes of ideas, each divided into subclasses and species. Each division had its separate sign, and these could be combined to form compounds. Parts of speech were indicated with precision and simplicity. The celebrated architect Christopher Wren presented Wilkins's idea to the Royal Society, which received it favorably (Shapiro 1969).

Inspired by the ideals of reason and optimism that swept Europe during the eighteenth century, many projects appeared, among them those of György Kalmar (1772) in Hungary, Christoph Berger (1779) and J. Z. Näther (1805) in Germany, and J. P. De Ria (1788) in Switzerland. Thanks to developments in linguistics, as well as in commerce, industry, and social theory, the tradition received fresh impulse in the nineteenth century. The Pasigraphical Society of Munich, for example, counted among its members the distinguished linguist Richter, the Egyptologist Lauth, and the diplomat Sinibaldo De Mas, who himself invented a pasigraphical system. In Paris in 1856, the International Society of Linguists came out for philosophical languages based on the principle of classification and for writing systems using this same principle. While authentic planned languages like Volapük and Esperanto were coming into being, pasigraphies continued to appear: Janne Damm (Leipzig, 1870), Stepan Baranovski (Kharkov, 1884), Joseph Orsat (Paris, 1910), Jakob Linzbach (St. Petersburg, 1916). A symbol system by S.A. Kukel-Krayevski appeared in 1921. Among more recent projects are Picto (K. J. A. Janson, 1957) and Antaŭ-Projekto (Jean Effel, 1968). Wsewolod Cheshikhin (1919) and Friedrich Robert Gilbert (1924) proposed the use of Chinese ideograms as a universal writing system.

PASILALIA

Pasilalia are audiovisual conventions generally employing letters, or sometimes signs, with a precise phonemic value, such that they can be combined into pronounceable words. They are universal languages in the true sense, in that they can be spoken as well as read. They can be classified, according to their relation to natural languages, as a priori or a posteriori languages.

A Priori Languages (metalanguages, schematic languages)

These languages are based on preconceived theoretical schemes and classifications, and not on the conscious imitation of natural languages. However, although their vocabularies appear to be the arbitrary inventions of their creators, it is remarkable that their grammars show little innovation and their authors remain content to simplify or systematize the grammars of national languages. The Indo-European grammatical categories are represented in nouns, adjectives, verbs, conjugation, declension, and so on, and the principles of word building for the most part reflect Indo-European morphology. Thus, Comenius (1592–1670) conjugates the root *ban-*'be' by means of suffixes showing person and prefixes showing tense:

present:	*bana*	*bane*	*bani*	*baná*	*bané*	*baní*
past:	*pabana*	*pabane*	*pabani*	*pabaná*	*pabané*	*pabaní*
future:	*fabana*	*fabane*	*fabani*	*fabaná*	*fabané*	*fabaní*

A Posteriori Languages (naturalistic languages, pseudolanguages)

These languages consciously imitate, in varying degrees, natural languages. Rather than classifying ideas in terms of some abstract "philosophical" order, they conform to the principles of existing languages, even as they simplify or regularize them. We can classify them according to their degree of resemblance to natural languages, using the term *naturalistic languages* for those closest to natural language.

The following examples illustrate the degree of resemblance between planned languages and natural languages:

French	*père*	*mère*
A priori planned languages:		
Letellier's project (1855)	*ege*	*egé*
Menet's project (1886)	*fat*	*tfat*
A posteriori planned languages:		
Volapük (1879)	*fat*	*mot*
Esperanto (1887)	*patro*	*patrino*
Ido (1907)	*patro*	*matro*
Interlingua (1951)	*patre*	*matre*

In C. A. Letellier's language, a root chosen arbitrarily to denote the family is given an inflection to specify various family relationships. In natural languages, of course, these relationships are expressed through different words. Different words are also used in the most naturalistic a posteriori languages, of which Interlingua is here the best example, but Volapük also has separate roots for 'father' and 'mother', derived from English. In Esperanto the root *patr-* and the feminine suffix *-in-* are drawn from natural languages, but Esperanto, unlike more naturalistic languages, derives the feminine systematically, by means of the same suffix. In this regard it resembles the projects of Charles Menet (who nevertheless uses a feminine prefix rather than a suffix) and Letellier, who derives the idea of mother from an anterior idea (father). There are national languages that use similar principles, but irregularly; thus Arabic *waalid* 'father' produces the form *waalida* 'mother'. Linguistic naturalism, an important principle in Ido and Interlingua, is accordingly a purely relative matter, useful for purposes of classification and not because of its semantic validity.

The classification of planned languages takes as its starting point the distinction between a priori and a posteriori languages— that is, between the tendency to schematize and the tendency to imitate or refer to natural languages. These tendencies are reflected in the word stock (artificial, natural, mixed) and in word building (purely a priori or displaying varying degrees of naturalism). Because of the great diversity of a posteriori languages, this classification lacks sufficient precision: as we have seen, some languages display both schematic and naturalistic traits, while others are difficult to classify because of their incompleteness. Bearing this caveat in mind, we can nonetheless categorize the over five hundred known projects in the following way:

I. A priori languages, characterized by largely artificial, non-ethnic word roots, schematic derivation, and fixed word categories (i.e., "philosophical" languages)
II. A posteriori languages
    A. Simplified ethnic languages (living or dead—i.e., minimal languages)
    B. Mixed languages using ethnic and nonethnic roots
        1. Schematically derived languages with ethnic word

roots in distorted form (e.g., Volapük) or with both artificial and ethnic roots (e.g., Perio, 1904)

    2. Languages with partly schematic and partly naturalistic derivation; ethnic roots of languages in this group are seldom or never distorted (e.g., Esperanto, 1887)

C. Naturalistic languages

    1. Languages with some schematic traits (Unial, 1903; Novial, 1928–1937)

    2. Languages with natural derivation (Occidental, 1922; Interlingua, 1951)

THE EVOLUTIONARY TRENDS OF PLANNED LANGUAGES

The history of planned languages from the seventeenth century to the present shows that a posteriori languages appeared late but spread quickly, while the a priori languages, after years of dominance, disappeared completely or were transformed into cybernetic languages. Because those who first became conscious of the language problem were philosophers and mathematicians, they sought the solution on their own territory, namely in logic, mathematics, semantics, and so on, using abstract methods; but they were little interested in the linguistic and practical aspects of the problem. Their projects imply that language is simply a concretization of preexisting mental structures, and thus they regard it not as a free-standing system but as dependent on the organization of mind. Their projects failed partly because they lacked a practical and easy solution to language barriers and partly because their authors sought solutions in what was in essence a blind alley.

However, among the philosophers a few achieved a remarkable level of sensitivity to language. John Wilkins (1614–1672) and Comenius (1592–1672) defined their projects in terms of a linguistic critique of Latin. Like their contemporaries, they tried to apply the "philosophical" method to their creations, but their analyses demonstrate a high degree of linguistic intuition. Comenius, for example, who wrote his treatise *Via Lucis* in England in 1641 and 1642, viewed Latin as benefiting only a limited number of educated people; its declensions, conjugations, syntax, and irregularities rendered it, in his view, inaccessible to the majority of the population. On the other hand, because

Italian had eliminated such difficulties, it had become popular in many nations, even among the Arabs and Turks. Comenius felt that a still more simplified language would achieve still wider use. Although he adhered to the Cartesian belief that a universal language might remedy the confusion of ideas and lead us to truth, Comenius did not lose sight of the linguistic side of things, returning constantly to questions of facility, precision, and beauty (Spinka 1943).

The earliest a posteriori language projects appeared around 1832, when the German F. A. Gerber published a long since forgotten project. In 1852 a project by Pedro Lopez Martinez appeared in Spain, and this was followed by Lucien de Rudelle's Cosmoglossa (1858) and Jean Pirro's Universalglot (1868). Here is an example of the latter:

> *Men senior, I sende evos un gramatik e un verb-bibel de un nuov glot nomed Universalglot. In futur I scriptrai evos semper in dit glot. I pregate evos responden ad me in dit self glot.*

> 'Sir, I am sending you a grammar and dictionary of a new language called Universalglot. In future, I will always write to you in this language. I request you to reply to me in this same language.'

Evidently, Pirro's aim was to create a synthesis of the principal European languages. The word roots are derived almost unchanged from Latin, Greek, German, English, French, and so on. Any impression of strangeness seems to come more from the association of roots and suffixes of different origins (e.g., the association of the German ending -*en* with the Latin root *respond*- to make the infinitive, or the French suffix -*rai* with the Latin participle *script*- to form the future tense) than from the various borrowings themselves, and the effect of artificiality results more from the general appearance of the language than from the alteration of borrowed words (*verb-bibel, glot, scripten*) or the creation of new ones (*men, evos*). Although Universalglot is for the most part formed from ethnic word roots, to European eyes it seems more artificial than Suma, an entirely a priori system created by Barnett Russell (1943) that gives a slightly exotic impression:

Sia sui te tima poti pito mote mi.

'She has left no message for you.'

We can accordingly conclude that a naturalistic language does not always look natural—a paradox that shows the difficulty of judging planned languages using the criterion of naturalism. As we have seen, this criterion is largely subjective and therefore relative. Nonetheless, it has played an important part in the development of planned languages. Comenius himself emphasized that a language must be beautiful, and this need for beauty caused the authors of language projects to imitate "nature" more and more. Although no serious attempt to define the concept was undertaken, *imitating nature* seems to have meant 'imitating existing ethnic languages'. This tendency was expressed in two ways: either through simplification of national languages or through the creation of syntheses of several ethnic languages.

SIMPLIFIED NATURAL LANGUAGES, OR MINIMAL LANGUAGES

Simplified Ancient Languages

One of the earliest examples is the macaronic Latin of Brother Théophile Folengo (1491–1544), but it is from 1880 on, following Volapük and in reaction to its excessive distortion of ethnic words, that projects to simplify or modernize Latin proliferate.[6] Between 1890 and 1892, George Henderson began publication of his journal *Nuntius latinus internationalis* in London. In Paris in 1901, Fred Isly launched his project Linguum Islianum. In 1902 both Karl Froehlich's Reform-Latein and Edward Frandsen's Universal Latein appeared in Vienna. These were followed by Giuseppe Peano's Latino sine flexione, which produced numerous offspring: Perfect (1910), Semi-Latin (1910), Simplo (1911), Novi Latine (1911), Latinulus (1919), Semprini's Interlingua (1922), Interlingua Systematic (1922), Unilingue (1923), Monario (1925), Latino Viventi (1925), Panlingua (1938), Mondi Lingua (1956).

Although simplified Greek had its supporters (among them Raymond Poincaré and, particularly, Raoul de la Grasserie in his Apolema of 1907), it never achieved the same level of popularity as simplified Latin. In fact the preference of authors of planned languages for Latin is an important aspect of their history. It shows that European linguists set great store by the criteria of beauty and naturalness, and it oriented the development of planned languages in the direction of imitation of Romance languages, to such an extent that it is often difficult to tell whether a given naturalistic language is a form of simplified Latin or is modeled on Romance languages. Consider the following translations of Ernest Renan's *Prière sur l'Acropole*:

> *Me e nasce, o Dea cum oculos caeruleo, de parentes barbaro, apud bono et virtuoso Cimmerianos, qui habita prope litore de mari obscuro....* [Latino sine flexione]

> *Io nasceva, o dea al oculos azur, de parentes barbare, inter le bon e virtuose Cimmerios, qui habita al bordo de un mare tenebrose....* [Interlingua, of IALA]

> 'I was born, O blue-eyed Goddess, of barbarian parents, among the good and virtuous Cimmerians, who live on the shores of a dark sea.'

Simplified Living Languages

The tendency of the stronger economic powers to seek control through economic expansion and the growth of nationalism inspired various projects for simplifying English, French, or Spanish, or creating inter-Germanic or inter-Slavic languages. In the Slavic territories under Austrian control, several pan-Slavic projects appeared, including those of Juraj Krizanić (1661), Blasius Cumerdei (1793), Joan Herkel (1826), Matija Majar (1865), Stanislav Tomić (1885), and Ignác Hošek (1908). Between 1888 and 1928, Elias Molee produced a series of projects for an American interlanguage based on English and German: Tutonish (1888), Niu Tutonish (1906), Allteutonic (1915), and Toito Spike (1923).

In Germany, first Lichtenstein in his Weltdeutsch (1853) and then Adalbert Baumann in his Wede (1915) proposed simplified versions of German to assist the spread of German culture. The name and date of Baumann's project are significant: *Wede, A Language for the Understanding of the Axis Powers and Their Friends. Munich, in the War Year 1915.* In 1928 Baumann published a modification with an equally significant title: *Oiropa*

Pitschn. The recent movement of the countries of western Europe into an economic union shows the pioneering nature of these projects. A project like Oiropa Pitschn is unsuitable for today because of its partisan goals and its national and racial bias, but the present functionaries of the European Economic Community are in general less language conscious than Dr. Baumann, having so far developed no coherent language policy, preferring, naively and chauvinistically, to try to force their own language on the others.

Spanish, with the Nuove Roman of Johann Puchner (1897), Italian, with Serafin Bernhard's Lingua Franca Nuova (1888), and Swedish, with K. G. Keyser's universal language (1918), also participated in the simplified language movement. Other than the simplified French of the German Johann Schipfer (1839), relatively few French projects were undertaken, though we should mention that of J. Giro (Paris, 1892), which probably inspired A. Lakidé's Fransezin (St. Petersburg, 1893) and Father Benjamin Bohin's Patoiglob (1898). On the other hand, it seems that numerous linguists recognized the extraordinary capacities of English. A few suggested merely superficial reform: Jonathan Swift (1711), James Bredshaw (1847), A. V. Starčevski (1890), Alexander Melville Bell (1888), R. E. Zachrisson's Anglic (1930), J. W. Hamilton's World English (1924). But an important project of great linguistic originality, revealing the remarkable flexibility of English, was C. K. Ogden's Panoptic English (1929), from which he derived Basic English (1935). (See Ogden 1930, 1934.)

Of all these attempts to create minimal universal languages by simplifying natural languages, living or dead, Basic English was the most conspicuous failure, because its emphasis on simplification so limited the language that it killed it. Bohin's simplified French (*le necesit, le concurans, lofr e le demand etr le loi des loi ci gouvern le mond*) seems shocking to the native French speaker because certain basic characteristics of French, such as gender and conjugation, are eliminated. English, with its more limited conjugation and lack of gender markings, does not suffer to the same extent by simplification. Thus Basic English is not particularly shocking to the English speaker, even though it is full of circumlocutions. Consider the following:

First, their countries seek no aggrandizement, territorial or other. [English]

First, their countries will do nothing to make themselves stronger by taking more land or increasing their power in any other way. [Basic English]

It is immediately apparent that the simplification in Basic English consists not in morphological distortion or in grammatical changes but only in semantic circumlocution: the vocabulary is simplified, not the individual words or the grammar. Hence Basic English conforms to the unconscious laws defining the aesthetic and spirit of the language. However, working with a mere 850 words, the user must constantly invent circumlocutions, which slow down expression and understanding. Furthermore, because new words cannot be created, there are few means to express nuances or to create poetic language. Basic English is certainly natural in appearance, but its capacity for expression is limited to what can be expressed in 850 words. In some respects it is more artificial than many of the so-called artificial languages.

Experiments with minimal languages revealed two principal defects: either they so disfigured the ethnic languages in question that they failed aesthetically, or they so limited expressive capacity that they failed as means of communication. In either case they betrayed their original by losing its uniqueness or its expressiveness. If a planned language is to become international, it must display as much morphological and syntactic beauty and as much semantic richness as an ethnic language. If so delicate and complex a creation is not quickly adopted by a community of users, the subjective biases of its author may easily destroy it. A language project may well be the work of an individual, but only its social acceptance and use will make it a language. This important conclusion came only late in the history of planned languages. It is well illustrated by the instructive history of Volapük, but no author of planned languages, except the author of Esperanto, has so far understood it.

VOLAPÜK

Johann Martin Schleyer, a Catholic priest from Baden, Germany, created Volapük in 1880, seven years before Zamenhof published Esperanto, at a time when awareness of the need for an international language was at its peak in Europe. In the preface to the first edition of his *Volapük: Grammar of a Universal Language for All Cultured Inhabitants of the Earth*, Schleyer offered the following, still relevant observations:

> Thanks to railways, steamships, telegraph and telephone, the world has shrunk in time and space. The countries of the world are in effect drawing closer to one another. Thus the time for small-minded and fainthearted chauvinism is forever over. Humankind becomes daily more cosmopolitan and increasingly yearns for unity. The amazing universal postal system is an important step toward this splendid goal. With respect also to money, weights and measures, time zones, laws and language, the brothers and sisters of the human race should move toward unity.

With unity in mind, Schleyer at first proposed a universal phonetic alphabet based on the Latin alphabet, with thirty-eight letters, by means of which, he believed, it would be possible to transcribe all languages. In this same connection he also proposed orthographical reform for German. In Volapük he retained only twenty-eight phonemes and took care to insure that their combination would be easy to pronounce, clearly audible, and aesthetically usable. His grammar was regular but difficult. There are four cases: nominative, genitive, dative, and accusative. Conjugation involves numerous prefixes and suffixes; thus 'I would have been loved' is rendered as *pilöfoböv* (p = passive prefix; i = pluperfect prefix; *löf* = the root 'love'; *ob* = first person singular; *öv* = suffix denoting the conditional. Although word roots are drawn from national languages, their form is so simplified that they are barely recognizable. 'World' becomes *vol*, 'speak' becomes *pük*, the German *Berg* becomes *bel*, and *haben* is rendered as *labön*. 'Animal' is *nim*, the adjective 'content' is *kotenik*. Affixes are used for word derivation: *pük* = 'language'; *gepük* = 'reply'; *lepük* = 'assertion'; *pükik* = 'linguistic'; *püköf* = 'eloquence'; *püköfav* = 'rhetoric'. Here is a sample:

> *Reidanes valik lüvipobs nulayeli läbikä benüköli. Dünobsös obs valik in vob kobik dini Volapükatikoda!*

> 'To readers we wish a happy and prosperous new year. May we all working together serve the cause of the universal language!'

Volapük spread rapidly among the middle class and intellectuals, to whom it was specifically directed. At the time, the Western middle class had no common means of understanding, since English had still not gained a dominant position over the other European languages. Only after the United States had established its economic superiority did financial and commercial circles adopt English, imposing it on their dependents. Volapük therefore appeared at the right moment. Because it was worked out in much greater detail than many other contemporary projects, it encountered immediate but ephemeral success. Within ten years, some twenty-five periodicals were appearing regularly, 283 Volapük societies had been founded, and textbooks existed in twenty-five languages. A standardizing academy was established, which soon began discussion of reforms. This was the critical moment that comes to all successful planned languages. Schleyer refused to compromise and rejected all suggestions for improvement. His intolerance caused first a schism and then collapse. The year was 1889; language projects were everywhere; a new one based on very different principles and ideas, called Esperanto, had just been born.

Volapük is important in the history of planned languages because it was the first to move successfully from theory to practice. Zamenhof acknowledged that Schleyer was the true initiator of the movement for an international language. In contrast to his predecessors, and even many of his successors, Schleyer tried to provide his language with a social foundation. Through the press, the Volapük societies, the academy, and numerous speeches, he gained a certain following among the public. But he did not understand that the shift from individual creation to collective practice implied self-sacrifice and tolerance appropriate to the spirit of a universal language. Schleyer's wish was that Volapük should remain not only the language of a cultured elite but also his own personal property. He defended his rights as author and opposed all change, even though his invention had already become a means of common expression and had entered the phase of collective development.[7]

For a further decade, Volapük continued to evolve in spite of Schleyer, but in a state of schism and disorder that proved suicidal. Modifications abounded: Emile Dormoy's Balta (1887), Nuvo-Volapük of Auguste Kerckhoffs (1887), Juraj Bauer's Spelin (1888), Fieweger's Dil (1893), Wilhelm von Arnim's Veltparl

(1896), A. Marchand's Dilpok (1898). It should be noted that these projects were increasingly naturalistic and Latin-based. In 1891 the Volapük Academy, torn among conflicting parties, elected Woldemar Rosenberger as its president. He moved its researches in a new direction; transformed into the Akademi Internasional de Lingu Universal, it developed the project Idiom Neutral (1902), which in turn passed through several reforms and emerged with a clearly Latin-based structure.

NATURALISTIC LANGUAGES

We have seen how, after it became clear that the purely "philosophical" languages (based primarily on seventeenth-century notions of reason) did not in fact work, the authors of language projects turned to naturalistic languages with varying degrees of schematization and with a growing bias toward Latin. This development was in line with the projects for minimal languages, among which those derived from Latin were the most numerous. Since 1887, the year of Esperanto's publication, most interlanguages have tended to belong not only to the Indo-European family but specifically to its Romance branch—a sign in itself of the extent to which Latin has influenced the civilization of Europe and America, where these planned languages came into being.

In 1887 the American Philosophical Society became interested in the question of a universal language and concluded that it should have the following characteristics: (1) the orthography should be phonetic, (2) there should be only five vowels (*a, e, i, o, u*), (3) it should be written with the Latin alphabet, (4) the grammar should be simple, and (5) the vocabulary should be drawn from Indo-European languages, primarily the Romance languages, not only because they were widely spoken but also because their lexicon could be easily assimilated.

This last observation was confirmed in 1888, when the author of Mundo-Lingue, the Austrian Julius Lott, having compiled a dictionary of seven thousand international words, noted that most of them were derived from Latin. In 1947 the International Auxiliary Language Association (IALA), which had been founded in 1924, submitted the results of its work to public scrutiny. Those questioned were asked to choose among four variations, and the people from non-Latin countries chose those that most resembled Latin. All important projects appearing after Esperanto, such as Jespersen's Novial (1928), Edgar von Wahl's Occidental (1922), Interlingua (1951), Romanid, by the Hungarian Zoltán Magyar (1956), and the various projects derived from Esperanto (Ido, 1907; Reform-Esperanto, 1910; Latin-Esperanto, 1911, and so on) have displayed a high degree of latinization.

At the same time, these projects reveal another evolutionary tendency: they are so naturalistic that they imitate the very arbitrariness and irregularity from which they were designed to escape. The term *naturalistic languages* is used for those a posteriori languages that, in addition to their tendency toward latinization, abandon the principles of fixity and schematization inherited from a priori projects: several graphemes represent various phonemes depending on their position in the word; a given grammatical category can be represented through various endings (for example, in Interlingua and Intal singular nouns can end in either a vowel or a consonant); roots have no fixed form, and so on.

If naturalism produces imitation of the defects of nature, it also returns, in the name of subjective aesthetic criteria, to complexity and confusion of the type that planned languages seek to eliminate. The phonetic system for such languages is not fixed. In Interlingua, for example, the letters *g*, *j*, *s*, *x*, *y*, and *z* represent two phonemes each, *c*, *ch* and *t* represent three, and the original pronunciation is allowed for certain borrowed words. Although it is easy for a European to read, in practice Interlingua can be used only as a written language, a role to which the pasigraphies were also limited and which any national language can play. At the same time, naturalistic morphology reintroduces irregularity within categories, rendering them recognizable only through their sense and not through their form. This implies that the problem of comprehensibility has been solved in some other way, since in all nonnaturalistic languages comprehensibility is primarily a function of fixity of form. In Volapük, for example, *e[Ent]lädob* can only be the first person singular (-*ob*) of the perfect indicative active (*e-*) of the verb *lilädön* 'to read'. While a language that is still essentially schematic, like Ido, uses only one affix for one function (e.g., *igar* 'to render in a certain way'), a naturalistic language like Mundo Lingue uses several synonyms: -*ificar*, -*efar*, -*ifar*, -*ilitar*, -*isar*. This variety produces neither facility nor simplicity, and it is unclear by what aesthetic or other advantage naturalism compensates for the loss of logical and regular derivation.

Universel (Menet)	Spelin	Esperanto	Interlingua	Italian	English
gov	yoebif	bovo	bove	bue	bull
ıgov	yobif	bovino	vacca	vacca	cow
govol	yubif	bovido	vitello	vitello	calf

ESPERANTO AND THE PLANNED LANGUAGES

Seeking to rationalize language, the first authors of planned languages tried to reduce it to a systematic classification of ideas. Important traces of such schematism are evident in Esperanto. The history of interlanguages began to develop rapidly, however, only when linguists became aware of the fact that the aim of language is spoken use. At this point purely oral criteria intervened, and the trend toward naturalism emerged from these criteria, with aesthetics in the lead. This explains in part the Latin nature of Esperanto and its successors, as well as the return to irregularity in the naturalistic languages. Although Esperanto borrows its lexicon from natural languages, its derivation and inflection retain a regularity and a schematic quality that clearly distinguish it from its naturalistic rivals.

No one has ever provided a serious definition of the criteria of naturalism. This being so, we might speculate as to whether it should be regarded as unnatural for a thinking being to create a rational and logical language. Arguably, such an activity conforms better to rational human nature, and hence is in itself more natural, than eternal dependence on so-called natural language. If we regard as natural only those attributes with which we are born, all the achievements of civilization become unnatural; thus we might declare all numbers—except one, two, and three—artifical because they do not exist in the most ancient languages.

Apart from psychological resistance to artificial language, which adds a pejorative nuance to the adjective *unnatural*, we can note that the essentially empty concept of unnaturalness was developed not during the rational seventeenth and eighteenth centuries but in the postromantic period in reaction to the rationality, universality and, in a word, classicism, of the previous centuries. Although the requirement of beauty is subjective, authors of planned languages must treat it as a psychological fact. It seems that a balance of aesthetic and rational tendencies produces a compromise between the schematic and the naturalistic. Esperanto puts this compromise into effect. Born in a period when Volapük was at its zenith, it profited from its predecessor's errors—and it was already fairly well established by the time the numerous projects for minimal latinized planned languages began to place increasing emphasis on naturalism.

The fact that Esperanto, alone among the planned languages, acquired a large community of speakers, merits special attention. Today it is used by individuals and social groups for a wide variety of purposes. Through Esperanto, students, professional people, travelers, scientists, and so on, not only satisfy the practical need to communicate, but also become aware of their own uniqueness and advantage compared with their fellows who do not use Esperanto. This awareness leads to the development of what might be described as a specifically Esperantist consciousness, and it is common to hear people refer to Esperanto as "their" language. The unique phenomenon of an artificially created but living language cannot of course be explained in linguistic terms alone. To study Esperanto in the same way as we studied any other language project—that is, from a purely linguistic point of view—would only partially account for its growing success. The aid of the psychologist and sociologist must be sought. Above all, we should explore why it was created and why it is increasingly learned in very different countries by very different social groups.[8]

The following chronology (table 1) presents only a few of the major projects. It helps to situate Esperanto in the history of planned languages and it emphasizes—

- the relative continuity of the various systems;
- the large number of mixed a posteriori projects since Volapük;
- the bias of authors of planned languages toward minimal languages between 1900 and 1935, when Basic English appeared as an insuperable technical success;
- the numerous naturalistic languages between 1922 and 1951;
- the Western character of interlinguistics;
- the contributions of the countries of continental Europe: Britain is underrepresented among the mixed a posteriori projects compared to France and Germany.

TABLE 1
A Chronology of Planned Languages.

Year	A Priori	A Posteriori Mixed	A Posteriori Naturalistic	Simplified	Pasigraphy
1876					Damm (D)
1879		*Volapük* Schleyer (D)			
1884	Maldant (F)				
1886					Baranovski (SF)
1887		*Esperanto* Zamenhof (PL)			Rosental (I)
1888		*Spelin* Bauer (YU)		*Germanic English* Molee (USA) *World English* Bell (GB)	
1889	*Spokil* Nicolas (F)		*Mundo Lingue* Lott (A)		
1892		*Balta* Dormoy (F)			
1893		*Dil*			
1896		Fieweger (D) *Veltparl* Von Arnim (D)			
1898		*Dilpok*			
1899		Marchand (F) *Langue Bleue* Bollack (F)			Hilbe (A)

(continued)

TABLE 1
(Continued)

Year	A Priori	A Posteriori Mixed	A Posteriori Naturalistic	Simplified	Pasigraphy
1902			*Idiom Neutral* Rosenberger (Russia)	*Tutonish* Molee (USA) *Latino sine flexione* Peano (I)	
1904	*Perio* Talundberg (D)			*Apolema* La Grasserie (F)	
1907		*Ido* Couturat (F)			
1908	*Ro* Foster (USA)			Hošek (CS) *Semi-Latin*	
1910		*Novesperanto* R. de Saussure (CH)		Moeser (A) *Simplo*	Orsat (F)
1911	*Molog* De Sarranton (F)			Ferranti (I) *Wede*	
1915		*Nepo* Cheshikhin (Russia)		Baumann (D)	
1916					Linzbach (Russia)
1918					
1920	*Beobi* Gordin (Russia)			Keyser (S)	
1922			*Occidental* Von Wahl (D)		
1925	*Loqa* Nield (F)	*Esperido* Raymond (USA)			

Year					
1927			*Novial* Jespersen (DK)		
1929				*Panoptic* Ogden (GB)	
1930				*Anglic* Zachrisson (S)	
1935			*Latinesco* MacMillan (GB)	*Basic* Ogden (GB)	
1943	*Suma* Russell (USA)	*Interglossa* Hogben (GB)	*Interlingua* I.A.L.A. (USA)		
1956		*Esperantuisho* Železný (CS); *Intal* Weferling (D)	*Romanid* Magyar (H)		
1957					*Picto* Janson (GB)
1961		*Neo* Alfandari (B); *Unilo* Jørgensen (DK)			
1963		*Malfalsito* Roussel (F)			
1965	*Unilingua* Agopoff (F)				

Abbreviations: A: Austria; B: Belgium; CH: Switzerland; CS: Czechoslovakia; D: Germany; DK: Denmark; F: France; GB: Great Britain; H: Hungary; I: Italy; PL: Poland; S: Sweden; SF: Finland Language names, where known, appear first, followed by authors' names.

Chapter 2

The Origins of Esperanto

LAZAR LUDWIK ZAMENHOF

Esperanto was a young man's creation. Lazar Ludwik Zamenhof was nineteen years old when he developed his first project for a universal language and twenty-eight when he published his first booklet (in Russian) *International Language* (1887), under the pseudonym Dr. Esperanto. From his earliest childhood he had been exposed to several languages, but under such painful circumstances that multilingualism seemed to him a largely negative phenomenon. In effect, the problem of linguistic diversity had already wounded his spirit before it came to occupy his intellect and intelligence. The city of Bialystok, where Zamenhof was born on 15 December 1859, is now in Poland. At the time it was situated in Lithuania, an area of the Russian Empire where ethnic groups and influences converged and mingled and which was constantly fought over and oppressed.[1] Zamenhof recalled his youthful experiences:

> The place where I was born and spent my childhood gave the direction to all my future endeavors. In Bialystok, the population consisted of four diverse elements: Russians, Poles, Germans and Jews; each spoke a different language and was hostile to the other elements. In this town, more than anywhere else, an impressionable nature feels the heavy burden of linguistic differences and is convinced, at every step, that the diversity of languages is the only, or at least the main cause, that separates the human family and divides it into conflicting groups. I was brought up as an idealist; I was taught that all men were brothers, and meanwhile, in the street, in the square, everything at every step made me feel that men did not exist, only Russians, Poles, Germans, Jews and so on. This was always a great torment to my infant mind, although many people may smile at such an "anguish for the world" in a child. Since, at that time, it seemed to me that the grown-ups were omnipotent, I kept telling myself that, when I was grown up, I would certainly destroy this evil.[2]

At home, Zamenhof used Russian, and on the street Polish. At school he learned German and French, Latin and Greek. His father, a competent Hebraist, taught him some Hebrew, and he may also have learned some Lithuanian. Yet it was neither his talent for languages nor his knowledge of them that led him to his interest in the language problem:

> Had I not been a Jew from the ghetto, the idea of uniting humanity would either never have come into my head or, if it did, would never have become a lifetime preoccupation. No one can feel the misery of barriers among people as strongly as a ghetto Jew. No one can feel the need for a language free of a sense of nationality as strongly as the Jew who is obliged to pray to God in a language long dead, receives his upbringing and education in the language of a people that rejects him, and has fellow-sufferers throughout the world with whom he cannot communicate. . . . My Jewishness has been the main reason why, from earliest

childhood, I have given my all for a single great idea, a single dream—the dream of the unity of humankind.[3]

Before leaving school in 1879, in the year Volapük was coming into being, Zamenhof completed his first effort at a planned language. He left it in the hands of his father when he went off to study medicine in Moscow and Warsaw. His father, a censor for the Jewish press, knew how dangerous would be the discovery, in the possession of a poor Jewish student, of papers written in a secret language. And so he destroyed his son's first project.

In Warsaw, where Zamenhof completed his studies, the czarist government constantly encouraged anti-Semitism at all levels of the population. In protest at such policies, the young man became active in the Zionist movement Khibat Zion from 1882 to 1887. These were years of poverty and hard work, during which he came to understand that a common language was not in itself enough to break down the barriers within society, and hence, while he worked on a new project for an international language, he also began to explore the idea of a universal religion.

What sets Zamenhof apart from all the other authors of planned languages is his own direct experience of social, racial, and religious conflict. He was not an ivory-tower linguist, out of touch with the concrete problems arising from, and expressed by, language differences. Human divisions and conflicts had caused him great suffering, and so he saw the creation of an international language as simply a first step toward a more general goal of peace. His actions were not motivated by personal vanity or national chauvinism (as was the case with some of the authors of universal languages) but directed at all those who suffered or were oppressed by language discrimination.

In 1886 Zamenhof completed his studies in ophthalmology, and in the following year he established a practice in Warsaw. That year, 1887, was also the year in which he married Klara Zilbernik and published his first booklet on his international language, first in Russian and then in Polish, French, German, and English. It contained some forty pages, thirty of which were devoted to a general introduction and the final pages to the "complete grammar" of the language.

In his preface, Zamenhof points out how much time, money, and energy must go into the learning of a foreign language. A common language would not only bring great savings, but it would also enrich humanity with the most outstanding cultural achievements of all nations. If we all learned two languages, our native language and the international one, we could devote more time to the first and deal with the cultures of the world in a spirit of full equality through the second. While the international language would facilitate contacts among scholars and business people, it would also eliminate the sense of foreignness among speakers of different languages. To date, Zamenhof wrote, pasigraphies had failed because they were too difficult and artificial languages had not caught the interest of the public. That was understandable: why give up one's time to learn a language spoken only by its inventor?

In response to these problems, Zamenhof set himself three goals: to make his language so easy that anyone could learn it for enjoyment, to make it immediately viable by giving it a logical and simple structure, and to find a way to stimulate the public into studying it in large numbers. He believed that he had found a way to guarantee the reader adequate reward for his or her efforts by including with his booklet eight sheets, each divided into four small forms with the following text: "Promise: The undersigned agrees to learn the international language proposed by Dr. Esperanto if it can be shown that ten million people have publicly made the same promise." In fact, only a thousand forms were returned to Zamenhof, and, in 1888, he published an address list with these first thousand addresses, thus beginning a tradition that remains today one of the most effective means of organization and public relations for the Esperanto movement.

Despite the government censor, the "international language" continued to gain popularity rapidly under the pseudonym of its creator: the first magazine in this new language, published in Nuremberg on 1 September 1889, was called *La Esperantisto*, (The Esperantist). In 1888 Zamenhof had produced *Dua libro de l'Lingvo Internacia*, (Second Book of the International Language) (Warsaw: Kelter). He wrote optimistically in the preface, "The numerous pledges that I have received, mostly signed 'without condition,' the letters of encouragement and advice—all these show me that my profound belief in humanity has not deceived me. The good genius of humanity has awakened. . . . Long live humankind, long live brotherhood among the peoples, and may these qualities live forever!" (*OV* 21).

In 1889 a supplement to the Second Book appeared. This was Zamenhof's last word as author of the language. From this point on, he considered the language not as his own property but as belonging to everyone. Its development would depend on all friends of the "sacred idea." For twelve years he himself had sacrificed much time and money for the "beloved cause," and if each of its enthusiasts would offer him a mere one percent of the effort, the goal would be rapidly attained. His emotional vocabulary shows how Zamenhof sought from the beginning to surround his language with high ideals. In his view, the language had to serve to "waken the good genius of humanity," to stimulate all energies into building a better world through unselfish cooperation.

The international language, then, was intended to play a role in the advancement of society and was associated with an almost mystical humanism of a kind that surfaced repeatedly during Zamenhof's lifetime and after. The point is important, since, although many Esperantists tried, even while Zamenhof was still alive, to eliminate from Esperanto any hint of ideology, the very name of the language encapsulated idealistic aspirations and served to inspire enthusiasm in generation after generation. We can certainly look at Esperanto from a purely linguistic point of view, but no purely linguistic examination of the phenomenon can explain its uniquely powerful attraction, its energizing powers, and its rich diversity.

Impoverished by the publication of his booklets and by family misfortunes, Zamenhof moved his practice several times before finally settling, in 1898, in a working-class neighborhood of Warsaw. During this period of relative poverty, he devoted himself to writing what proved to be his most important contributions to the future of the language. In 1894 his *Universala vortaro* (Universal Dictionary) appeared, with translations of each word in five languages. This was followed by the *Ekzercaro* (Exercises) and in 1903 by the *Fundamenta krestomatio*, an anthology that brought together the previously published Exercises, and articles, lectures, stories, poetry, and prose, both original and translated. In 1905 came the aptly named *Fundamento de Esperanto* (Foundation of Esperanto), containing a sixteen-rule grammar, the Exercises, and the dictionary of 1894 (see Zamenhof 1905).

Published eighteen years after the initial booklet, the

Fundamento fixed the canon of the language. The Esperanto movement, which now spread all across Europe, accepted it immediately. In August 1904, 180 Esperantists, most of them from Britain and France, met in Calais and accepted an invitation from the Esperanto group in the Channel port of Boulogne-sur-Mer to attend the First World Congress of Esperanto. It opened in Boulogne on 5 August 1905, with 668 participants from twenty countries. A few days earlier, Zamenhof had received the Legion of Honor from the French Minister of Public Instruction.

The Boulogne Congress began the tradition of World Congresses of Esperanto and was followed by congresses in Geneva (1906), Cambridge (1907), Dresden (1908), Barcelona (1909), Washington (1910), Antwerp (1911), Krakow (1912), and Bern (1913). A total of 3739 people registered for the 1914 congress, planned for Paris, but the meeting could not take place due to the outbreak of hostilities. The tradition was renewed in 1920, but again interrupted from 1940 to 1947 by World War II. It has continued ever since from year to year and country to country.

Zamenhof did not live to see the end of the First World War. Worn out by work and deeply depressed by the disintegration of his ideal of peace, he died on 14 April 1917, having jotted his last thoughts on paper: "I have begun to feel that perhaps death is not disappearance . . . that there exist certain laws in nature . . . that something guides me to a higher end" (*OV* 358).[4]

ZAMENHOF'S IDEAL

This "higher end" was the reconciliation of humankind. It runs through all Zamenhof's writings. Its origins lie in the principles of brotherhood and equality, as he makes clear in his speech before the Boulogne congress:

Brothers created on a single pattern, brothers with similar ideas, with a similar God in their hearts, brothers who should have helped one another and worked together for the happiness and glory of the human family—these brothers have become strangers to one another, they have divided themselves, apparently forever, into hostile camps, and among them an everlasting war has begun.

Zamenhof went on to say that prophets and poets have dreamed of a time when unity would come, but this has remained nothing more than a dream. Now, for the first time, thanks to the international language, the dream was beginning to come true. People from different countries understood one another, and conversed like brothers and sisters—not like French talking to English, or Russians talking to Poles, but human beings talking with human beings.

But Zamenhof warned that this brotherly and sisterly spirit could not be fully realized unless peoples and social classes dealt with one another in full equality. An artificial language has the advantage of not offending national chauvinists: it humbles no one and acknowledges the fundamental equality of all ethnic languages. "In our meeting," Zamenhof asserted before a gathering of Esperantists, "there are neither strong nations nor weak, neither privileged nor underprivileged; no one is humiliated, no one is made uneasy. We all stand on the same neutral footing, the rights of all are fully equal, we all feel ourselves members of a single nation, members of a single family" (*OV* 361–62).

Zamenhof understood that an international language brings with it a profound democratization of culture and communication. In his essay "The Essence and Future of the Idea of an International Language," presented to the French Association for the Advancement of Science (Paris, 1900), he addressed directly the question of the link between Esperanto and democracy: "Every natural language, both living and, particularly, dead, is so terribly difficult that only people with a great deal of free time and financial resources can really learn it thoroughly." If a natural ethnic language were to be adopted as a means of international communication, "we would not have an international language in the true meaning of the word, but simply an international language for the higher social classes . . . whereas with an artificial language, everyone, not just the intelligent and the rich, but all spheres of human society, even the poorest and least educated of villagers, would be able to master it within a few months" (*OV* 299). While only the "select classes" are able to master the ethnic languages, because they have the necessary time and money, an international planned language belongs to the people at large.

This declaration contains within it, then, a clear-sighted

critique of elite culture, based on wealth and power, and it correctly emphasizes the fact that by their very nature the ethnic languages stand in the way of the acquisition of international culture by the mass of ordinary people. Only a language that can be acquired by the poor and the uneducated will serve to democratize culture and communication. The goal of an international planned language is to allow direct communication among the masses without the required mediation of the elite and the ruling classes—in sum, to allow the masses to free themselves, at least as far as language is concerned, from their dependence on the privileged classes.

To make this language easier to learn and use than ethnic languages, and, at the same time, to guarantee the same degree of expressive power and aesthetic grace, Zamenhof built it on logical rules, without exceptions, as the philosophers of the seventeenth century had recommended, and he sought maximum internationality in pronunciation and vocabulary, while at the same time avoiding the temptation of naturalism, which tends to reintroduce arbitrariness and exceptions. We will see later how he applied these principles, but we should note here that he prepared the way for the collective development of the language, an approach fully in accord with his democratic temperament. Zamenhof reproached the creator of Volapük for having stood in the way of the development of his creation through his authoritarian stance. Zamenhof himself, from the very beginning, renounced all rights to his language. He submitted proposals for reform to the Esperantists, accepted their verdict, and always regarded himself as a simple user of Esperanto among all the others.

Clearly, then, for Zamenhof the creation and practice of an international language was aimed primarily at stimulating people's idealistic tendencies toward a sense of universal brotherhood. In his famous letter to Alfred Michaux, he wrote:

> This idea is the essence and goal of my entire life. My work for Esperanto is only part of this idea. I never stop thinking and dreaming of the other part, and, sooner or later (perhaps very soon), when Esperanto no longer needs me, I shall come forward with a plan that I have been preparing for some time. . . . This plan (which I call "Hillelism") involves the creation of a moral bridge by which to unify in brotherhood

all peoples and religions, without creating any newly for-
mulated dogmas and without the need for any people to
throw out their traditional religions. My plan involves creating the kind of religious union that would gather together all
existing religions in peace and into peace—in much the
same way as a kingdom might gather together various
separate principalities, obliging none to surrender its own
separate traditions. [*Let* 1:107]

Having published a Russian-language brochure in Warsaw
(1901) under the Latin pseudonym *Homo sum* (I am a human)
and entitled Hillelism, in 1906 he again set forth his ideas in an
anonymous article, "Beliefs of Hillelism" (*Dogmoj de hilelismo*), in
the journal *Ruslanda esperantisto*:

Hillelism [named after the rabbi Hillel, a contemporary of
Jesus] is a doctrine that, without separating a person from
his native country, or language, or religion, gives him the
possibility of avoiding all untruths and antagonisms in the
principles of his national religion and of communicating
with people of all languages and religions on a basis that
is neutrally human, on principles of common brotherhood,
equality and justice. [*OV* 316]

Zamenhof defines this doctrine as follows:

1. "I am a human being, and for me there exist only purely
   human ideas."
2. "All peoples are equal, and I judge all people on their personal
   value and actions, not on their origins."
3. "Every country belongs not to this or that people but to all its
   inhabitants with fully equal rights."
4. "Every attempt by one person to force on others his language
   or religion I regard as barbarism."
5. Patriotism involves service to all fellow citizens and not just
   the majority.
6. In every country every language and religion should have
   equal rights, regardless of whether it is that of the majority or
   the minority.
7. Religion is based on three principles: (a) God is that unknow-
   able force that rules the world; (b) its fundamental rules

should be "Do unto others as you would have them do unto you" and "Listen always to the voice of your conscience"; (c) since religious customs come from humans, not from God, Hillelists should aim for ever greater unity. [*OV* 316–21]

It is clear that the situation of the Jews of central Europe strongly influenced this doctrine for the defense of minorities that Zamenhof was later to rename *homaranismo*. Although it met with little favor, and sometimes resistance, from Western Esperantists, Zamenhof worked hard to disseminate it. In 1913 he published in Madrid a somewhat larger booklet, *Homaranismo*, and began preparations for a congress in Paris in the summer of 1914 to establish the foundations for this "religion in the making."

The word *religion* is somewhat misleading, since *homaranismo* was neither creed nor theology, but rather a "neutrally human" doctrine directed above and beyond religious differences, toward the common aspirations of all people. It sought to put the concept of humanity above those of nation, ethnic group, race, class, and religion.

The sudden outbreak of war ruined Zamenhof's plans, and the entire project for a neutral faith failed to outlive its author. But it is important because it helps us understand what Esperanto meant for him. From the start the international language was not only a rational solution to problems of communication but also the emotional reaction of a sensitive spirit to persecution and blind hatred in an uneducated and benighted society. Although Esperanto's development was quite separate from any ethical or philosophical system, it preserved a certain emotional commitment and an idealism that set it apart from other language projects, which tended to limit themselves to the purely mechanical side of linguistics and were thus reduced to mere codes.

Compared to other authors of planned languages, Zamenhof was an innovator because he was acutely aware of the simple fact that a language is an instrument with a purpose, and not the purpose itself. For this reason he linked Esperanto closely with Hillelism: "An international language," he wrote in a letter to Beaufront in 1906, "has the goal of creating among the people a neutral bridge with respect to language. *Homaranismo* seeks to do it in all other ways. *Homaranismo* is simply a stronger form of Esperantism" (*OV* 337). He also understood that the language not only serves a particular purpose, but that the purpose serves the language: "Just as Hillelism cannot exist without an international language," he wrote to Abraham Kofman in May 1901, "so the idea of a neutral language will never really come about without Hillelism!" (*OV* 323). There is truth in these prophetic words: the success of Esperanto or any other planned language depends on the "feeling" that carries it from place to place,[5] in other words on the high ideal, however we describe it, that gives it life.

ESPERANTISM

Would Esperanto become the language of a sect or group of ideologues? When Zamenhof arrived in Boulogne-sur-Mer for the first World Congress of Esperanto, the local organizers prudently elected to avoid any too obvious expression of religiosity or politics. They feared that the voice or tone of a Jewish prophet in a country alternately rational and bigoted would provoke sharp criticism or deadly ridicule. They did not prevent Zamenhof from giving expression to his hopes, but they redirected the congress toward the narrower issue of linguistic communication through a Declaration on the Essence of Esperantism, which dissociated the language from all ideologies:

> Esperantism is an effort to disseminate throughout the world the use of a neutrally human language, which, "without interfering in the internal affairs of individual peoples and in no way seeking to dislodge the existing national languages," would afford people of different nations the possibility of mutual understanding; which would also serve as a pacifying language for public institutions in those countries where various nations quarrel among themselves about language, and in which there might be published those works of common interest to all peoples. All other ideas or aspirations which the individual Esperantist may attach to Esperantism are a purely private matter, for which Esperantism is not responsible. [*OV* 237]

The following year, the Geneva congress adopted a Declaration on the Neutrality of Esperanto Congresses, inspired by the declaration of Boulogne. The name Esperantist, it was agreed, might be given to "all the people who know and use Esperanto, regardless of the purpose for which they use it." While the general acceptance of the international language would have, at some point in the future, important consequences for the "political, religious and social" lives of the peoples of the world, "these consequences will be achieved only through major reforms in current institutions and customs." Esperantists might have differing views on the nature of these changes, but because the ultimate transformation of society depended above all on Esperanto's success, it was essential to work together for the victory of the international language. For this reason disputes and disagreements should be avoided; accordingly the neutrality and harmony of the congresses had to be guaranteed. So congress programs "must not allow the discussion of political, religious and social questions" in general meetings; those interested in such issues could discuss them among themselves only in private meetings (*Let* 1:287–88).

This declaration, through which the Esperantists and even Zamenhof himself refused to commit Esperantism to any one ideology, philosophy, or religion (including Hillelism), sought to ensure the coexistence of all points of view. Yet, whereas Zamenhof viewed neutrality and universality as a dynamic synthesis of these points of view, the declaration conceived of them as a balance among unrelated philosophies. Because the slightest shift endangered that balance, neutrality of this latter kind soon led to immobility, and in turn to schism, because by implication it raised a fundamental question about the purpose of an international language: A language for what? Can it hope to move forward without any more powerful motivation than practical communication? Should one learn it only for immediate profit or in the hope of future "consequences" for the "lives of the peoples of the world"? Although even today the question of the purpose of Esperanto is still not fully resolved, probably even the most strictly neutral of Esperanto groups share some sense of common idealistic goals. This typical Esperantist ideal is the so-called internal idea.

THE INTERNAL IDEA

Zamenhof proclaimed the Internal Idea at the same congress that accepted the declaration of neutrality. Although he fully subscribed to the definition of Esperantism adopted in Boulogne-sur-Mer, he emphasized that Esperanto possessed, in addition to its practical utility, an optional yet fundamental philosophy. An Esperantist, Zamenhof agreed, is anyone who uses the language, regardless of the purpose for which that person uses it. No one may force an ideal on the language, but that in itself "gives no one the right to insist that we see Esperanto only as a practical affair." Some people maintain that Esperanto is just a language and that we must avoid linking it with any other idea, even privately, for fear of offending people.

> What words! Out of fear of offending those people who want to use Esperanto only for practical purposes, we are asked to tear out of our hearts that part of Esperantism that is most important, most sacred—the idea that is the central aim of the Esperanto cause, that is the star that has always guided all fighters for Esperanto! Oh no, no, never! We protest and reject such a requirement. If we, the first to join the fight for Esperanto, are forced to avoid doing anything that involves ideals, we would rather tear up and burn everything we have written in support of Esperanto, we would rather destroy the work and the sacrifice of a lifetime, painful though it would be.... We would cry in disgust, "With that Esperanto, made to serve only commercial aims and practical utility, we want nothing in common!" [*OV* 371–72]

There will come a time, says Zamenhof, when the language will lose its ideological character because of its worldwide acceptance, but in the meantime the motivating force of Esperantism remains "the sacred, grand and important idea that an international language contains in itself... brotherhood and justice among all peoples" (*OV* 372). If Zamenhof had sacrificed the greater part of his life for Esperanto, it was not for material satisfaction:

> If, as often happens, people confined to their deathbeds write to me that Esperanto is the only consolation of their final days, are they then preoccupied with its practical utility? No, no, no! They have in mind the internal idea contained in Esperantism. They value Esperanto not because it unites people's brains but because it unites their hearts. [*OV* 373]

What would Zamenhof have said had he known the degree of sacrifice to which many Esperantists would carry their dedication to this internal idea in prisons and concentration camps thirty years later![6]

The Boulogne and Geneva declarations on the neutrality of Esperantism protected it against the influence of outside ideologies but did not silence its specific message. Zamenhof inspired the movement with a particular kind of idealism, emphasizing the progressive and evolutionary potential contained in an international language simply by virtue of its internationality. He presented Esperanto as a new and decisive factor in the transformation of the social order to create a better world, and he called for cooperation in the struggle to bring this about. The learning and use of Esperanto, he argued, would raise the social consciousness of individuals and groups and bring them together purely by virtue of their common humanity. Esperanto was addressed, then, to the noblest aspirations of the human race and sought to mobilize these aspirations. At the same time it brought concrete rewards because all who learned it were aware that they were contributing to human progress. In a word, the language could motivate the lives and actions of those individuals capable of considering the long term, rather than short-term selfish concerns.

As we have already mentioned, the history of Esperanto reveals a succession of examples of heroic devotion and sacrifice. As with other great political and religious ideals, the Internal Idea was capable of raising the individual above personal concerns, releasing altruistic tendencies and channeling them into the realization of a concrete social goal. Once again, in Cambridge in 1907, on the occasion of the third world congress, Zamenhof insisted that this goal was one of brotherhood and freedom and that Esperanto congresses in effect constituted prototypes of a new world order. All Esperanto activities arise from the certainty that Esperantists work not for their personal gain but for the benefit of all. "Why, then, are we meeting?" asked Zamenhof. To discuss questions of language? To practice speaking? To bring Esperanto to the attention of the public? "Yes, for these reasons certainly! But since of every hundred participants at least ninety-nine derive from Esperanto only moral profit, why are we bringing it to the public's attention? I do not doubt that most of you will give me only one reply: we are demonstrating Esperantism not because of the utility that any of us personally derive from it, but because of the common significance that Esperantism has for all humankind.... Just as the ancient Hebrews, three times a year, used to gather in Jerusalem, to rekindle in themselves their love for the idea of a single God, so we, each year, gather in the capital of the land of Esperanto to rekindle the idea of Esperantism. And this is the main principle and main aim of our congresses." (*OV* 377)[7]

Being an Esperantist does not depend on the purpose for which one uses the language, but if a person wishes to attend a congress or join an organization "which carries the green flag,"[8] that is, incorporates the true Esperanto idea, that person, says Zamenhof, must put aside all private political, religious, or social attitudes and conform to the internal idea: "In the realm of Esperanto the language Esperanto is not the only guiding principle, but also the idea of Esperantism.... The motto of such Esperantists ... is: 'We wish to create a neutral foundation on which the various ethnic groups might communicate with one another in peace and brotherhood, without forcing on one another their ethnic differences'" (*OV* 378–79). Thus Zamenhof implicitly distinguishes between "utilitarian" Esperantists and those motivated by the "idea" that constitutes "the realm of Esperanto" among the Esperantists. The latter type are those who are the conscious seeds, as it were, of the social order to be founded on brotherhood, justice, and freedom: the Internal Idea and *homaranismo* are rooted in the same ground. Although Esperanto congresses, organizations, and institutions have long since gone over to a more utilitarian, practical position, the Esperantists themselves for the most part continue to feel that they constitute, from generation to generation and from country to country, a kind of diaspora conscious of its fundamental unity—what Zamenhof called an Esperanto people.

THE DEVELOPMENT OF ESPERANTISM

From the beginning Zamenhof's ideal was not universally accepted, and even among those who accepted it, some did so only partially. But thanks to this ideal, Esperanto became, in Zamenhof's words at the Krakow congress, not only a language among languages but "an important social issue." In comparison to the other language projects, Esperanto acquired an emotional quality and a strong appeal: "the most beautiful dream of humankind" is related to all those other constantly recurring myths that help people along by locating the golden age of the world in the future. Although reason and common sense argue for the acceptance of a universal language and there are many scientific reasons for favoring Esperanto, it is not reason and science that generally cause people to become Esperantists.

It is interesting to observe the evolution of the internal idea in relation to the sociological development of Esperantism. In the initial, founding period of Esperanto, up to the First World War, the ideology of the movement remained strongly influenced by that of Zamenhof. But the tension between the primarily linguistic and primarily idealistic attitudes to the language and the problem of their interrelatedness forced Zamenhof and other prudent leaders to look for equilibrium in a neutrality generally in sympathy with the Internal Idea. After the war and the founder's death, the movement entered a new phase, of consolidation and organization, in which it adapted itself to the changed international circumstances and defined its goals accordingly. More than ever the ideal of peace was important, though this ideal grew more general also among non-Esperantists because of the sufferings of the war, as the establishment of the League of Nations shows very clearly. The similarity of goals between the league and Esperantism obliged the latter to define itself more distinctively, namely as a movement devoted to solving the problem of language differences, with which the league was not concerned. From then on, the Esperanto movement tended to emphasize this aspect as its principal social function, with the intention of demonstrating the practical advantages of Esperanto for peace.[9]

For similar reasons, since the Second World War the specifics of Esperantism have tended to move further away from the ethical toward the linguistic side. The establishment in 1954 of Consultative Relations between UNESCO and the Universal Esperanto Association brought the Esperanto movement closer to official organizations with similar fundamental principles.[10] Because the Internal Idea was recognized by these organizations, at least with respect to the ideals of justice and brotherhood, Esperantism was once again obliged to insist on its linguistic goals. In today's Esperanto movement there exists a marked tendency to see Esperanto as a phenomenon separate from all ideologies and not necessarily related to any moral or social ideal. The representatives of this tendency shift the Internal Idea of the movement to non-Esperanto institutions (organizations, political parties, societies, and the like) and compensate by putting greater emphasis on the value of Esperanto for linguistic communication. In this way they put their language on the same level as all others and consider Esperantology simply as another branch of linguistics.

Their scholarly approach to the language has clearly shown the linguistic and educational merits of Esperanto. As an object of academic research, Esperanto now appears in a modern dress that is easier for the public to accept. It has also gained in reputation as it has succeeded in removing or muting the odder and more emotional manifestations of "greenness". It is, after all, wise to adapt one's public relations and recruitment to suit the public's changing styles and patterns of thought.

But we should not confuse adaptation with conformity. The systematic persecution of Esperantists before, during, and after the Second World War under various dictators shows that to these people Esperanto was more than a language. If the words *fraternity* and *justice* have become such a common part of political rhetoric that they now sound totally innocuous, internationalism is another matter, especially since the founding of the workers' and the so-called non-national Esperanto associations (see chap. 6). Because this popular version of the Internal Idea coincided with the ascendancy of the English language and the power of the United States, financial and economic leaders turned more and more to English and ceased supporting the Esperanto movement. Their lack of faith in an international language of the people, added to the fact that they have adopted English internationally and no longer need a new means of communication among themselves, finds expression in the official attitudes of the Western democracies toward Esperanto. Although the language is not strong enough to impress government authorities, they tend to fear it because of its potential.

We remember, sadly, to what shameful degree (for example in the 1930s) some Esperantists humiliated themselves to appease nationalist tendencies—vainly. It is doubtful whether anything of the language or movement would remain if the Esperantists were to give up their unique characteristics. Can Esperanto prosper in foreign soil—without the Internal Idea, which so inspired its creator and kept the movement alive through such an eventful period of history? Why should the ideals of peace and brotherhood be reserved for official institutions, which have so far not adopted Esperanto, while Esperanto is one viable means of achieving peace? Certainly the Esperantists should apply tact and realism in their development of the full potential of the language, but they should above all not forget that potential, which constitutes their historical and social uniqueness.

Chapter 3

The Language

FORMATION AND STABILIZATION

The Fundamento

Although Zamenhof composed several projects between 1878 and 1887, only a few sample lines of the first project and some fifteen fragments from 1881 survive. These scant remains, however, allow us to trace the development of the broad traits of the final project and to discern how linguistic intuition based on experimentation resolved certain hesitations and reduced Zamenhof's concessions to Volapük (Waringhien 1959: 19–48). With the publication of his 1887 booklet, Zamenhof did not claim to have permanently fixed the shape of Esperanto. Searching for improvements, he freely submitted the language to the criticism of his correspondents and to the readers of *La Esperantisto*, the earliest Esperanto magazine. During the six years in which this magazine appeared, from 1889 until the czarist censor halted its entry into Russia in 1895, its articles examined various modifications and reforms in the language, some of which—including the suppression of certain consonants, abandonment of the accusative ending and adjectival agreement, and modification of certain suffixes—show that Zamenhof was willing to depart radically from his original conception.

Having founded a League of Esperantists consisting of all the subscribers to *La Esperantisto*, Zamenhof asked them to choose between an unmodified Esperanto and a version reformed in line with the earlier discussions. Out of this mail ballot there emerged a majority (157 respondents) opposed to any change. Ninety-three voters declared that they would welcome minor modifications, but only fourteen voted for fundamental changes. Zamenhof accepted this verdict. Although many subscribers gave him their ballots to use as he saw fit, he took no advantage of this opportunity to impose his own opinion on the Esperantist community. He himself abstained from voting.

In 1905 Zamenhof published, in Paris, the *Fundamento de Esperanto*, which perpetuated the language in its 1887 form. Since the Boulogne congress, the *Fundamento* has remained the basic grammatical reference for Esperantists. According to paragraph 4 of the famous Declaration on the Essence of Esperantism, accepted in Boulogne, "The single foundation of the language Esperanto, obligatory, once and for all, for every Esperantist, is the *Fundamento de Esperanto*, in which no one has the right to make changes."

The aim of the *Fundamento*, as presented in Zamenhof's preface to the work, is not to prevent all further evolution but rather to protect the language against the anarchy and arbitrariness of possible individual or group initiatives. Zamenhof certainly favored the enrichment of the language through the introduction of neologisms, but he did believe that the language could survive only if it developed in accordance with clearly defined and obligatory principles. These principles were to remain inviolate until the day arrived when Esperanto achieved official recognition in the world and legal guarantees protected it against individual caprice. At that time, an international committee chosen by the various governments would have the right to introduce all the changes deemed necessary. Until then, everything contained in the *Fundamento* was to be compulsory for all users of Esperanto, including its inventor.

The Sixteen Rules

Though a degree of dogmatism was certainly useful in preserving the integrity of Esperanto, Zamenhof's intention was simply to provide a means of orientation and a framework for the possible further development of the language. The Sixteen Rules of the *Fundamento* provide that framework. In the context of these "rules," a more detailed linguistic description is possible and of course desirable.

1. There is no indefinite, and only one definite, article, *la*, for all genders, numbers, and cases.
2. Nouns are formed by adding -*o* to the root. For the plural, -*j* must be added to the singular. There are two cases: the nominative and the objective (accusative). The root with the added -*o* is the nominative, the objective adds an -*n* after the -*o*. Other cases are formed by prepositions.
3. Adjectives are formed by adding -*a* to the root. The numbers and cases are the same as in nouns. The comparative degree is formed by prefixing *pli* 'more'; the superlative by *plej* 'most'. 'Than' is rendered by *ol*.
4. The cardinal numerals do not change their forms for the different cases. They are: *unu, du, tri, kvar, kvin, ses, sep, ok, naŭ, dek, cent, mil*. The tens and hundreds are formed by simple junction of the numerals. Ordinals are formed by adding the adjectival -*a* to the cardinals. Multiplicatives add the suffix -*obl*; fractionals add the suffix -*on*; collective numerals add -*op*; for distributives the word *po* is used. The numerals can also be used as nouns or adverbs, with the appropriate endings.
5. The personal pronouns are: *mi, vi, li, ŝi, ĝi* (for inanimate objects and animals), *si* (reflexive), *ni, vi, ili, oni* (indefinite). Possessive pronouns are formed by suffixing the adjectival termination. The declension of the pronouns is identical with that of the nouns.
6. The verb does not change its form for numbers or persons. The present tense ends in -*as*, the past in -*is*, the future in

-*os*, the conditional in -*us*, the imperative in -*u*, the infinitive in -*i*. Active participles, both adjectival and adverbial, are formed by adding, in the present, -*ant*-, in the past -*int*-, and in the future -*ont*-. The passive forms are, respectively, -*at*-, -*it*-, and -*ot*-. All forms of the passive are rendered by the respective forms of the verb *esti* (to be) and the passive participle of the required verb. The preposition used is *de*.

7. Adverbs are formed by adding -*e* to the root. The degrees of comparison are the same as in adjectives.
8. All prepositions take the nominative case.
9. Every word is to be read exactly as written.
10. The accent falls on the penultimate syllable.
11. Compound words are formed by the simple junction of roots (the principal word standing last). Grammatical terminations are regarded as independent words.
12. If there is one negative in a clause, a second is not admissible.
13. To show direction, words take the termination of the objective case.
14. Every preposition has a definite fixed meaning, but if it is necessary to use a preposition, and it is not quite evident from the sense which it should be, the word *je* is used, which has no definite meaning. Instead of *je*, the objective without a preposition may be used.
15. The so-called foreign words (words that the greater number of languages have derived from the same source) undergo no change in the international language, beyond conforming to its system of orthography.
16. The final vowel of the noun and the article may be dropped and replaced with an apostrophe.[1]

Fundamental though they may be, these rules alone cannot describe the language adequately. Esperanto cannot be reduced to such a skeletal structure: like all living languages, it has its own complex autonomy. Accordingly, we must apply to it the same methods of investigation as we would use for any living language. Zamenhof expressed his linguistic concepts in the terminology of the grammars of the various national languages then available in Europe, all of them conforming to the Latin model. If this model was suitable for describing the Romance languages, it worked less well for the others. But it was only in the 1950s that grammarians in various countries launched a general offensive against Latin-derived concepts. Even today they continue to be widely taught, and words like *verb, noun, adjective, adverb, preposition*, to say nothing of the word *word* itself, are known all across the world. It is important to note that Zamenhof intuitively perceived an entirely different mode of conceptualizing and presenting grammar, as we shall see shortly, and that he conformed to contemporary terminology largely for obvious didactic and public-relations reasons.[2] For similar reasons, the following description of Esperanto will follow largely conventional grammatical terminology. Let us begin with a specimen text.

Text

> Cetere en la nuna tempo en la afero de lingvo internacia la rutino kaj spirita inercio iom post iom komencas cedadi al la sana prudento. Jam longe tie aŭ aliloke en diversaj gazetoj kaj revuoj aperas artikoloj plenaj de aprobo por la ideo mem kaj por ĝiaj batalantoj. Sed tiuj ĉi artikoloj estas ankoraŭ senkuraĝaj, kvazaŭ la aŭtoroj timas, ke oni elmetos ilin al publika malhonoro. Tiuj ĉi senkuraĝaj voĉoj perdiĝas en la laŭtega ĥoro de la kriistoj kaj mokistoj, tiel ke la grandega plimulto de la publiko, kutiminta iradi nur tien, kie oni krias la plej laŭte ... ĉiam ankoraŭ rigardas la ideon de lingvo internacia kiel sensencan infanan fantazion. Tiun ĉi publikon konvinki ni ne entreprenas, ĉar ĉiuj niaj vortoj pereus vane. Ĝin konvinkos nur la tempo. [*OV* 279–280]

Phonetic Transcription

> tsɛ'tɛrɛ ɛn la 'nuna 'tɛmpɔ ɛn la a'fɛrɔ dɛ 'lingvɔ intɛrna'tsia la ru'tinɔ kai spi'rita inɛr'tsiɔ kɔmɛntsas 'iɔm pɔst 'iɔm tsɛ'dadi al la 'sana pru'dɛntɔ. jam l'ɔngɛ 'tiɛ au ali'lɔkɛ ɛn di'vɛrsai ga'zɛtɔi a'pɛras arti'kɔlɔi 'plɛnai dɛ a'prɔbɔ pɔr la i'dɛɔ mɛm kaj pɔr 'dʒiai bata'lantɔi. sɛd 'tiui tʃi arti'kɔlɔi 'ɛstas an'kɔrau sɛnku'radʒai 'kvazau la au'tɔrɔi 'timas. kɛ 'ɔni ɛl'mɛtɔs 'ilin al pu'blika malhɔ'nɔrɔ. 'tiui tʃi sɛnku'radʒai 'vɔtʃɔi pɛr'didʒas ɛn la lau'tɛga 'xɔrɔ dɛ la kri'istɔi kai mɔ'kistɔi 'tiɛl kɛ la gran'dɛga pli'multɔ dɛ la pu'blikɔ kuti'minta i'radi nur 'tiɛn 'kiɛ ɔni 'krias la plɛi 'lautɛ 'tʃiam an'kɔrau ri'gardas la i'dɛɔn dɛ 'lingvɔ intɛrna'tsia 'kiɛl sɛn'sɛntsan in'fanan fanta'ziɔn.

'tiun t∫i pu'blikɔn kɔn'vinki ni nɛ ɛntrɛ'prɛnas t∫ar 't∫iui 'niai 'vɔrtɔi pɛ'rɛus 'vanɛ. dʒin kɔn'vinkɔs nur la 'tɛmpɔ.

Translation

Furthermore, at the present time the routine and the spiritual inertia in the matter of an international language are beginning gradually to give way to healthy common sense. For a long while, here and there in various magazines and journals, articles have been appearing, full of approval for the idea itself and those fighting for it. But these articles are still without courage, as though the authors fear that they will be exposed to public dishonor. These voices, lacking courage, are lost in the chorus of professional mockers and shouters, so that the great majority of the public, accustomed to going only where people shout loudest . . . still invariably regards the idea of an international language as a senseless, childish fantasy. This public we do not undertake to convince, because all our words would perish in vain. It will be convinced only by time.

PHONOLOGY

Alphabet

a [a]	*b* [bɔ]	*c* [tsɔ]	*ĉ* [t∫ɔ]	*d* [dɔ]	*e* [ɛ]	*f* [fɔ]
g [gɔ]	*ĝ* [dʒɔ]	*h* [hɔ]	*ĥ* [xɔ]	*i* [i]	*j* [jɔ]	*ĵ* [ʒɔ]
k [kɔ]	*l* [lɔ]	*m* [mɔ]	*n* [nɔ]	*o* [ɔ]	*p* [pɔ]	*r* [rɔ]
s [sɔ]	*ŝ* [∫ɔ]	*t* [tɔ]	*u* [u]	*ŭ* [wɔ]	*v* [vɔ]	*z* [zɔ]

Pronunciation

Esperanto's orthography constitutes an almost perfect phonological representation of the system of phonemes because each grapheme represents a single phoneme. The five vowels, *a, e, i, o, u* (respectively /a/, /ɛ/, /i/, /ɔ/, /u/), form two series:

$$\begin{array}{ccc} \text{/i/} & & \text{/u/} \\ \text{/ɛ/} & & \text{/ɔ/} \\ & \text{/a/} & \end{array}$$

with the possible variation:

```
         i              u
            e      o
               a
```

Thus we hear ['bela] and ['bɛla], ['fɔrmɔ] and ['foto], depending on the national origin of the speaker.

Esperanto also contains six descending diphthongs:

aj/ai/	*ej*/ɛi/	*oj*/ɔi/	*uj*/ui/
aŭ/au/	*eŭ*/ɛu/		

The grapheme *ŭ* appears only in diphthongs as a sign of an unaccented phoneme /u/. At the beginnings of words it is used only to transcribe the semivowel /w/, as in *Ŭagadugu.*

As for the consonants, they include two virtually symmetrical series of voiced and unvoiced phonemes:

unvoiced:	*s*	*c*	*ŝ*	*ĉ*
voiced:	*z*		*ĵ*	*ĝ*

These consonants resemble those in the following English words:

s = **see**
c = **bits**
ŝ = **she**
ĉ = **chair**
z = **zero**
ĵ = **pleasure**
ĝ = **gem**

There is also the semivowel *j* (pronounced like an English *y*), an aspirated *h* and velar *ĥ* (pronounced as in the German *Bach*), although the latter is often replaced with a *k*: *arĥitekto* = *arkitekto*; *meĥaniko* = *mekaniko.*

Accent

Accent is fixed, falling on the penultimate syllable of each word. Since the final -*o* of nouns and -*a* of the article can be elided, the prosody of the language can shift from amphibrach (x/x) or trochaic (/x) rhythm to iambic (x/) and anapestic (xx/). It has been calculated that about two-thirds of the words are amphibrach

Table 2
Consonants in Esperanto.

	Labial	Labiodental	Dental	Alveolar	Palatal	Velar	Glottal
Stops	p		t			k	
	b		d			g	
Affricates			c	ĉ			
				ĝ			
Fricatives		f	s	ŝ		ĥ	h
		v	z	ĵ			
Nasals	m		n				
Laterals				l			
Trills				r			
Glides (semivowels)	ŭ				j		

and one-third trochaic. Elision permits much greater rhythmic diversity, widely used in poetry and oratory.

espero	x/x
esper'	x/
malesper'	xx/

MORPHOLOGY

Esperantologists generally distinguish three essential classes of morphemes in the language: roots, affixes, and grammatical endings. Kalocsay and Waringhien describe them as follows:

1. The roots are syllables or groups of syllables that indicate some concept, object or notion (*hom, bel, kur*).
2. The affixes are syllables which limit or modify the meaning of the root to which they are attached but have no influence on its grammatical character or on its word-building function. . . . These affixes can be suffixes or prefixes. . . .
3. The endings are sounds which come at the end of all Esperanto nouns, adjectives and verbs, and of all adverbs except the primitive [invariant] adverbs. [1981: 371–72]

Using this taxonomy, we can analyze the word *nesanigebla* 'incurable' in the following way:

ne-   prefix (prefixed negative adverb)
san-   root common to the adjective *sana*, the noun *sano*, the verb *sani*, and the adverb *sane*
-ig-   causative or factitive suffix (aspectual suffix) meaning 'to make, render, cause to be'
-ebl- suffix (suffixed adjective) indicating possibility
-a   adjective ending

This mode of analysis, while convenient, insufficiently clarifies the originality of Esperanto, as it is described by Zamenhof himself:

> I have arranged the language to allow for the *analysis* of ideas into independent words, so that the entire language, instead of consisting of words in various grammatical forms, is made up exclusively of *unchanging* [invariant] words. If you take a text written in my language, you will find that every word appears *always* in one invariant form *only*, namely in that form in which it is printed in the dictionary. And the various grammatical forms, the reciprocal relations among the words, and so on, are expressed through the combination of invariant words. But because a linguistic structure of this kind is entirely foreign to European peoples and it would be difficult for them to grow used to it, I have presented this analytical aspect of the language in a completely different way, in conformity with the spirit of the European languages, so that anyone learning my language with a textbook, without having read the introduction first (which is quite unnecessary to the learner), would not even imagine that the construction of this language differed from his or her mother tongue. The word *fratino*, for example, in reality consists of three words: *frat* 'brother', *in* 'woman', *o* ('something that is, or exists') (= that which is a brother-woman = 'sister'). But the textbook explains *fratino* as follows: 'brother' is *frat*, and it ends in *-o* because all nouns end in *-o* in the nominative, hence *frat'o*; to indicate the female form of this same idea, we add the small word *in*, hence *frat'in'o*; and the apostrophes are added to show the constituent

grammatical parts of the word. In this way the analytical nature of the language in no way embarrasses the student; he does not even suspect that what he calls an ending or a prefix or a suffix is, in fact, an entirely free-standing word, which carries the same meaning whether it comes at the beginning or end of another word or stands on its own; that every word can be used equally as a root-word or as a grammatical particle. [Zamenhof 1903: 234–35; emphasis in original]

This text is the only place in which Zamenhof describes the linguistic theory that he used to create his language. It is important both because of its innovative character and because it sums up the essence of Esperanto. Zamenhof explains that Esperanto consists of independent and invariant words. These words maintain the same form and remain autonomous regardless of their place in the sentence; furthermore, they can be used as roots or as grammatical words.

This linguistic theory was born of a purely practical need: the need to create a language immediately comprehensible to someone who has not met it before. The pasigraphies provided Zamenhof with an analogy, as he explains to Borovko:

Finally, the so-called secret alphabets, which do not require that the entire world learn them in order for them to work, but allow an addressee entirely unacquainted with them to understand everything written to him, as long as he has the key—these alphabets led me to the idea of arranging the language in the form of such a "key," which might contain not only the entire vocabulary but also the complete grammar in the form of separate, free-standing and alphabetically arranged elements, thus providing an addressee, of whatever nationality, unacquainted with the language, a way of immediately understanding a letter written to him. [*OV* 421–22]

These important texts show that Zamenhof conceived of his language as a combination of indivisible and independent units. Following André Martinet, we shall call these minimal "free-standing elements" monemes. They differ in terms of their role in the sentence. Lexemes are words carrying meaning—that is, they show the general significance: *sun, teler, manĝ, util, ĵus, hodiaŭ,* and so on. Morphemes are instrumental words showing the relations among the lexemes: *o, as, j, n, de, al,* and so on. Different scholars use different terminology. Some use the word *morpheme* to cover both categories, distinguishing between lexical morphemes (roots) and grammatical morphemes (affixes, endings, articles, prepositions, etc.). This terminology works equally well, provided we do not overlook the fact that in Esperanto all linguistic units are constituent parts of the lexicon, whether they carry meaning or merely grammatical value. Furthermore, these distinctions are useful primarily to describe the linguistic system, that is, to define the various combinations and their corresponding functions among the basic units.

Lexemes

Seventy-five percent of the lexemes in Esperanto come from Romance languages, primarily Latin and French; 20 percent come from Germanic languages; the rest include borrowings from Greek (mostly scientific words), Slavic languages, and, in small numbers, Hebrew, Arabic, Japanese, Chinese, and other languages. The increasing introduction of scientific and technical terms is raising the number of Greek and Latin roots, but in no way lessens the practical importance of the Germanic elements, which include a large part of the basic vocabulary: *telero, glaso, forko, suno, tago, vintro, jaro, fingro, trinki,* and so on. Furthermore, the Latin lexemes tend to be chosen because of their internationality, and hence perhaps 40 percent are immediately comprehensible to a Slav.

Compared to other planned languages, the basic vocabulary of Esperanto displays a reasonably satisfactory balance among the various Indo-European languages, in proportion to their actual occurrence in international relations. The fact that the vocabulary is Indo-European in no way signifies that the structure of the language has the same origins. What is more, the large number of Latin roots (fewer, however, than in Ido or Interlingua) is more an advantage than a disadvantage if we bear in mind that English, so far the most international of the national languages, draws over half its words from the Romance languages and that only 25 percent of its vocabulary can be described as native. Esperanto stands midway between those naturalistic projects that draw their lexicon from a single language or group of languages, and certain mixed languages like Veltparl (1896), Pankel (1906), and Cosman (1927), which consider internationality to consist in the greatest possible diversity of sources.[3]

When compared to those of other constructed languages, the lexemes in Esperanto reveal two principal characteristics. First, they are monomorphic. In this respect Esperanto differs from naturalistic languages, which, imitating natural languages, frequently permit dimorphism or polymorphism. Thus, while Occidental alternates the roots *vid-* and *vis-* in the words *vider*, *vision*, *visibilita*, Esperanto derives all these concepts from a single lexeme, *vid-* (*vidi*, *vido*, *videbleco*).

Second, words borrowed from other languages retain their integrity. While Volapük distorted its lexical borrowings, we can always identify the source of a lexeme in Esperanto. Most lexemes enter Esperanto from ethnic languages without change. The French *commencer* or English *commence* becomes *komenci*; the Latin *timere* becomes *timi*; German *laut* becomes *laŭta*; Russian *khor* becomes *ĥoro*; Greek *kai* becomes *kaj*. The rare instances where modification does take place are dictated by necessity, namely—

- to avoid homophony. For example, the German *locken* becomes *log-* to avoid confusion with the Latin *locus* (*lok-*), and the English *lava* becomes *laf-*, to distinguish it from *lav-*, derived from the French *laver*.
- to avoid confusion between monemes and morphemes (lexical and grammatical morphemes). *Cigarette* becomes *cigaredo* so that its ending is not confused with the suffix *-et-*, which indicates diminution; the German *Rubin* becomes *rubeno* because the suffix *-in-* denotes the feminine; and the Latin *vigilis* becomes *vigla* because the suffix *-il-* denotes an instrument for doing something.
- to avoid polysemy, or multiple meanings for a single word. For example, the different meanings of the French *accorder* are rendered as *akordi* and *agordi*, and those of *boucle* as either *buko* or *buklo*; the English 'to drink' can be rendered as *trinki* or *drinki*, the latter meaning 'to drink to excess'.
- to achieve greater internationality. For example, *lavango* 'avalanche' is derived from both the German *Lawine* and the Italian *valanga*.

• very occasionally, to make words simpler. For example, the Russian *nepremenno* is rendered in Esperanto as *nepre*.

Such alterations occur seldom and prudently. Except in a few cases, they do not distort the original word but apply phonological principles similar to those in ethnic languages, such as vocalic transformation (French *récolte* becomes Esperanto *rikolto*), apheresis (French *esprit* becomes Esperanto *sprito*), or abbreviation (Latin *quantitas* becomes Esperanto *kvanto*).

If we now compare Esperanto lexemes with those of natural languages, we are immediately struck by the fact that lexical processes are fundamentally different in Esperanto. What students of Esperanto call roots do not always correspond to the phenomena described by that term in ethnic languages. While it is true that, in many cases, the parallel is precise (*land-o*/*Land* [German], *vid-i*/*vid-ere* [Latin], *ĉerp-i*/*ĉerp-at* [Russian], *ĉu*/*czy* [Polish]), in other instances the "root" unites several lexical morphemes (monemes) and coincides with what in an ethnic language would be called a radical. Thus, in *inspir-i*, the root *inspir-* has lost the Latin distinction between the root *spir-* and the prefix *in-*, so that the two constitute a single lexeme, yet *elspir-* and *enspir-* are divisible into two elements, namely *el-spir* and *en-spir*. As this example shows, in Esperanto the roots do not refer back to the etymology of their sources but constitute new unities. Hence there are a few lexemes of strongly related, or even identical, etymology (such as *ag-*, *akt-*, *aktor-*, *akci-*) which must nonetheless be regarded as independent and unrelated lexemes. Something similar occurs with respect to the French word *utile*, where the root *ut-* is joined with the suffix *-ile* in the single radical *utile*. In the same way, in the English word *answer*, the root *swear* is no longer distinguished from the prefix *and-* but unites with it to form a single radical.

Zamenhof's originality lay in presenting his lexicon not as a list of words (lexes) but as a list of lexemes, or significant units. In French, the words *main*, *manier*, *menotte*, and *manuel* constitute four distinct lexical units, or lexes, in which the lexeme *man-*/*main* is associated with differing suffixes. Following Hebrew lexicologists, Zamenhof exploited the fixed form of his lexemes as a dictionary device, classifying under each of them the lexes derived from them. Thus, under *man* he classified *mano*, *mana*, *maneto*.

Efforts have been made to discern grammatical characteristics in Esperanto lexemes, and scholars have sought to classify
them as verbal or as nominal (nouns, adjectives, and pronouns),
based on the translations Zamenhof provided in five other
languages (French, English, German, Russian, Polish) in the
Universala Vortaro, for example:

> *aĉet-: acheter / buy / kaufen / pokupat' / kupować*
> *acid-: aigre / sour / sauer / kisly/ kwasny*

According to some grammarians, *aĉet-* is a verbal lexeme because
it is translated by a verb, and *acid-* is nominal because it is translated by an adjective. However, we cannot regard translation as a
linguistic criterion. To be understood by the public, Zamenhof
had to translate the Esperanto lexemes using words from ethnic
languages, but that does not prove that he wished to indicate
anything more than the general meaning. The distinction between verbal and nominal lexemes applies categorical concepts
to Esperanto that prove only vaguely definable. One of the major
achievements of modern linguistics has been to prove that the
traditional categories of nouns, verbs, adjectives, and so on, are
not necessary to describe every language—in other words, that
they are not universal concepts. For this reason it seems counter-
productive to impose them on a language of universal purpose
such as Esperanto. We can say, then, that in Esperanto the
lexemes belong to no fixed grammatical category, but that they
constitute categorized words (lexes), either verbal or nominal,
when a verbal or nominal morpheme, indicating the grammatical
function, is added to them.[4]

Lexemes	Lexes (words)
rapid-	*rapid-a* 'fast', *rapid-o* 'speed', *rapid-e* 'rapidly', *rapid-i* 'to make haste, go fast'
sap-	*sap-o* 'soap', *sap-a* 'soapy', *sap-e* 'in a soapy fashion', *sap-i* 'to soap'
batal-	*batal-i* 'to fight', *batal-o* 'battle', *batal-a* 'having to do with combat', *batal-e* 'in battle'
jes	*jes* 'yes', *jes-o* 'consent, agreement', *jes-a* 'affirmative', *jes-e* 'affirmatively', *jes-i* 'to approve, affirm'

In theory, there exists no limit to this system; in practice, the only practical limit is semantic. Theoretically, there could exist verbs like *mi-i* or *is-i*; they would be neither morphologically nor syntactically monstrous, but simply semantically not immediately understandable—primarily because in many ethnic languages the corresponding notions do not exist. Verbs like *isti*, *ismi*, *peri*, *igi*, *avari*, and *feliĉi* are entirely logical, even though we could not form equivalents in ethnic languages. Because of the nongrammatical character of many of its lexemes, English is more accommodating in this respect than most languages, hence such pairs as *eye* and *to eye*, *run* and *to run*, *fish* and *to fish*. This shows that, even though the ethnic languages may contain numerous idioms that are hard to render in comprehensible universal concepts, Esperanto is rich in another way, namely in its almost limitless capacity to build words in universal categories.

Grammatical Morphemes

Characterizers. In certain cases a morpheme (moneme) may carry a lexical morpheme indicating its grammatical class or function. Certain morphemes appear without categorizer: flexible lexemes (*iu* and its series, *ia* and its series, *io* and its series: see Correlatives, below), inflexible lexemes (numbers, all elements in a compound word except the last, as in **okulvitro**, **manlabori**), inflectional morphemes (personal pronouns, nominal and verbal flexives: see Inflections, below), and particles (see below). Other morphemes are followed by a characterizer (*o* for nouns, *a* for adjectives, *e* for adverbs). For verbs there is no single characterizer: it is determined by inflection (*-i, -as, -is, -os, -us, -u*: see Inflections, below). The infinitive indicator *-i* can be classified under verbs or nouns, depending on our definition of the infinitive. We should note that these characterizers indicate grammatical class. Thus a lexeme normally carrying no characterizer takes a characterizer when it changes class: *mi → mia, dek → deko → deka*. Likewise, a lexeme carrying a characterizer changes it when the class changes: *deko → deka; fino → finis*. However, since the grammatical function does not always receive a specific function indicator, the class indicator can serve as a function indicator: *-o* shows that the word in question is a noun and also that the noun is in the subjective or prepositional case: *la komenco estas bona; je la komenco.*

Inflections. We can distinguish three categories of inflections: nominal, verbal, and verbal-nominal. Concerning nominal inflections we can note that—

- plurals are indicated with the ending *-j*. There is no plural form for verbs (*Tiuj senkuraĝaj voĉoj perdiĝas* 'Those timorous voices are lost').
- case (accusative; illative, or accusative of entry; allative, or accusative of direction) is indicated by the ending *-n* added to nouns, adjectives, pronouns, and adverbs ending in *-e*. *Ili rigardas la ideon.* 'They consider the idea'. *Iradi tien, kie . . .* 'to keep going (in the direction of) there, where . . .'. *Nur la tempo konvinkos ĝin.* 'Only time will convince it'.
- gender relates only to nouns. There is a suffix only for the feminine: *vir-o, vir-in-o* (cf. Hebrew *ish, isha*), *patr-o, patr-in-o* (cf. Arabic *waalid, waalida*). In this regard Zamenhof anticipated the modern theory of glossematics, which analyzes the morpheme morphosemantically, beyond the limit of the sign, defining *woman* as 'man' + 'she' (cf. *virino* = *viro* + *ŝi*; *patrino* = *patro* + *ŝi*).
- the indefinite pronoun makes a distinction between the neuter (*io* and its series) and the masculine and feminine (*iu* and its series). See Correlatives, below.
- the personal pronoun distinguishes the three genders in the third person singular (*li, ŝi, ĝi*) but not in the plural (*ili*).

Verbal inflections can be classified as indicative (present, past, future—respectively, *-as, -is, -os*), conditional (*-us*), infinitive (*-i*), and imperative (*-u*), as in the following examples:

> *mi estas* 'I am'
> *mi estis* 'I was'
> *mi estos* 'I will be'
> *mi estus* 'I would be'
> *esti* 'to be'
> *estu* 'be!'

A third category of inflections can be described as verbal-nominal. Since verbs do not change according to person, only the preceding noun or pronoun provides this indication, as shown in table 3.

TABLE 3
Pronouns.

	First person	Second person	Third person		
Singular	*mi*	*vi* *ci* (poetic)	*li*	*ŝi*	*ĝi*
			si (reflexive) *oni* (indefinite)		
Plural	*ni*	*vi*	*ili*		
			si (reflexive) *oni* (indefinite)		

Only the participles distinguish between perfective and non-perfective aspect, as in table 4:

TABLE 4
Participial Aspect.

Participle	active	nonperfective	-ant-	*batalanto*: the fighter in the act of fighting
			-ont-	*batalonto*: a person about to fight
		perfective	-int-	*batalinto*: a person who was fighting
	passive	nonperfective	-at-	*legata libro*: a book in the process of being read
			-ot-	*legota libro*: a book about to be read
		perfective	-it-	*legita libro*: a book which has been read, which one has finished reading.

In Zamenhof's usage, these inflections do not combine with verbal inflections. Nothing in Zamenhof's theory, however, argues against such forms as *mi dormintus* 'I would have slept', *mi dormantas* 'I am sleeping', or *mi venkitas* 'I am conquered'.[5]

- The inchoative shows the beginning of an action and is indicated by the prefix *ek-* (*ekparoli* 'to begin to talk').

- The durative, indicating a prolonged or continual action, is indicated by the suffix *-ad-* (*parolado* 'a speech'; *agadi* 'to continue to act').
- The causative is indicated by the suffix *-ig-* (*venigi iun* 'to make someone come'; *lumigi ion* 'to make something light up').
- The translative, indicating a change of state, is rendered by *-iĝ-* (hence *malsani* 'to be sick', but *malsaniĝi* 'to become sick'; *blankiĝi* 'to become white').

Table 5 shows how the verb (0) can be transformed in two pivotal directions: along the axis 1–3 (causative-translative) or along the axis 2–4 (inchoative-durative):

TABLE 5
Verbal Transformations.

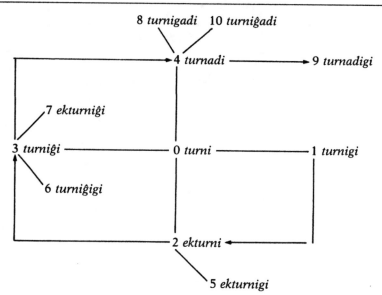

0. *turni* = 'to turn' (transitive)
1. *turnigi* = 'to make to turn'
2. *ekturni* = 'to begin to turn'
3. *turniĝi* = 'to turn' (intransitive; i.e., 'to be turned')
4. *turnadi* = 'to continue to turn'
5. *ekturnigi* = 'to make (someone, something) begin to turn (someone, something)'
6. *turniĝigi* = 'to make someone turn around'
7. *ekturniĝi* = 'to begin to turn' (intransitive)

(continued)

TABLE 5
(*Continued*)

8. *turnigadi* = 'to continue to make to turn'
9. *turnadigi* = 'to make (someone, something) continue to turn'
10. *turniĝadi* = 'to keep turning around'[6]

Correlatives. Inspired by the schematism of the "philosophical" language projects, Zamenhof constructed nine series of five morphemes to perform certain so-called correlative functions. The first morpheme in each series is simple and indefinite, and the other four are derived from it with the aid of a particular initial consonant. Four of these series are pronominal or adjectival and five are adverbial. The pronominal-adjectival series follows:

TABLE 6
Pronominal-Adjectival Correlatives.

	Individual Pron.-adj.	Quality Adj.	Thing Pron.	Possessor Pron.
Indefinite	*iu* 'someone' 'some' (adj.)	*ia* 'some kind of'	*io* 'something'	*ies* 'someone's' 'something's'
Interrogative	*kiu* 'who' 'what' (adj.)	*kia* 'what kind of'	*kio* 'what'	*kies* 'whose'
Demonstrative	*tiu* 'that person' 'that' (adj.)	*tia* 'that kind of'	*tio* 'that thing'	*ties* 'that person's' 'that thing's'
Collective	*ĉiu* 'everyone' 'every'	*ĉia* 'every kind of'	*ĉio* 'everything'	*ĉies* 'everyone's' 'everything's'
Negative	*neniu* 'no one' 'no'	*nenia* 'no kind of'	*nenio* 'nothing'	*nenies* 'no one's' 'nothing's'

Note that—
- the *-iu* and *-ia* series take the accusative (illative, allative) and plural inflections;
- the *-io* series has no plural;
- the *-ies* series is invariable;
- the semantic difference between the *-iu* and *-ia* series is that *-iu* indicates identity, and *-ia* indicates quality.

TABLE 7
Adverbial Correlatives.

	Quantity	Place	Time	Cause	Manner
Indefinite	*iom* 'some amount'	*ie* 'somewhere'	*iam* 'sometime'	*ial* 'for some reason'	*iel* 'somehow'
Interrogative	*kiom* 'what amount'	*kie* 'where'	*kiam* 'when'	*kial* 'why'	*kiel* 'in what way'
Demonstrative	*tiom* 'that much'	*tie* 'there'	*tiam* 'then'	*tial* 'for that reason'	*tiel* 'in that way, thus'
Collective	*ĉiom* 'every amount'	*ĉie* 'everywhere'	*ĉiam* 'always'	*ĉial* 'for all reasons'	*ĉiel* 'in all ways'
Negative	*neniom* 'no amount'	*nenie* 'nowhere'	*neniam* 'never'	*nenial* 'for no reason'	*neniel* 'in no way'

Derivations.   There are two principal forms of derivations: prefixes and determinatives (the so-called suffixes, which are affixed to the lexemes before the grammatical indicators). Occasionally, more than one prefix or more than one determinative may be affixed to a lexeme (e.g., *remiskalkuli* 'to miscalculate again', *misrekalkuli* 'to make an error in recalculating'; *dikuleto* 'a small fat person', *diketulo* 'a plumpish person'). In these instances, the outermost affix governs the remainder of the word.

Prefixes

bo-	relation by marriage: *bopatrino* 'mother-in-law'
ge-	both sexes: *gepatroj* 'parents', *gesinjoroj* 'ladies and gentlemen'
dis-	dispersion, separation: *disdoni* 'to distribute', *disiri* 'to go separate ways'
mal-	opposite: *malhonoro* 'dishonor', *malbona* 'bad'
mis-	involving an error: *miskalkuli* 'to miscalculate'
pra-	antiquity: *prahistorio* 'prehistory', *prapatro* 'ancestor'
re-	repetition, reciprocation: *rekonstrui* 'to reconstruct, rebuild', *redoni* 'to give back'
retro-	reverse direction: *retroiri* 'to go back'

Determinatives
(These are sometimes added at the end, sometimes inserted into a word.)

-aĉ-	pejorative: *ridi* 'to laugh', *ridaĉi* 'to cackle'
-aĵ-	concretizer: *alta* 'high', *altaĵo* 'high place'
-ar-	collective: *arbo* 'tree', *arbaro* 'forest'
-ec-	abstract: *bela* 'beautiful', *beleco* 'beauty'
-eg-	augmentative: *belega* 'very beautiful', *altega* 'very high'
-ej-	place: *lerni* 'to learn', *lernejo* 'school'
-end-	obligation: *lernenda* 'that must be learned'
-et-	diminutive: *beleta* 'pretty', *lerneti* 'to learn a little'
-ind-	worthiness: *leninda* 'worth learning', *ridinda* 'laughable'
-ist-	profession: *instrui* 'to teach', *instruisto* 'teacher'
-obl-	multiplicative: *du* 'two', *duobla* 'double'
-on-	fraction: *duono* 'half'
-op-	numerical collective: *duopo* 'a group of two, pair'
-ul-	person: *riĉa* 'rich', *riĉulo* 'rich person'
-um-	an indefinite suffix denoting some kind of link between the root and the word: *plena* 'full', *plenumi* 'to fulfill', *aero* 'air', *aerumi* 'to air'

In addition, there are two modifiers of endearment or familiarity: *-nj-* for the feminine and *-ĉj-* for the masculine. These are different from the other suffixes in that they are not necessarily added to the last syllable of the lexeme: *patrino* 'mother', *panjo* 'mommy', *patro* 'father', *paĉjo* 'daddy'.

Within their semantic limits, the various derivatives may be combined with one or more characterizers, thereby becoming independent words: *ge/gea, dis/dise, mis/mise, mal/malo, aĉ/aĉa, re/ree*. Many words are formed in this way: *aĵo* 'thing', *aro* 'group, collection', *eco* 'quality', *ejo* 'place', *ege* 'greatly', *eta* 'tiny', and so forth. In this way morpheme and lexeme are gradually moving together. While Zamenhof distinguished the suffix *-ej-* from the lexeme *lok-*, *-eg-* from *mult-*, *-ec-* from *kvalit-*, *-ar-* from *grup-*, and so on, modern usage tends to regard them as synonyms and it is now unclear whether such compounds as *lernejo, pafilego*, or *esperantistaro* are derived words (i.e., derived from lexemes by means of suffixes) or compound words (i.e., associated lexemes). Confusion of this kind between lexeme and morpheme remains impossible in many cases: *pafilego*, in the Esperanto of Zamenhof's day, is not a 'big gun', nor is *altaĵo* a 'high thing'; *rideti* is different from *iom ridi* and *viveti* from *iom vivi*. But in other instances the "lexemization" of grammatical morphemes is clear: *anaro* (*an-ar-o*), *enirejo, admirinda, klerulo, etulino* (*et-ul-in-o*).

Particles. We can note the following types of particles in Esperanto:

- The article: *la*: *la tablo, la tablon, la tabloj*
- Underived adverbs: in addition to the above list of correlatives we should add such adverbs as *nun* 'now', *hodiaŭ* 'today', *tuj* 'immediately', *ĵus* 'just', *hieraŭ* 'yesterday', *baldaŭ* 'soon', *morgaŭ* 'tomorrow', *jam* 'already', *ne* 'no, not', *jes* 'yes', *ja* 'indeed', *eĉ* 'even', *pli* 'more', *plej* 'most', *nur* 'only', *tre* 'very', *tro* 'too', etc.
- The interrogative particle *ĉu*.
- The demonstrative particle *ĉi* (*ĉi tiu libro* 'this book').
- Connectives. They are of four kinds: conjunctions, prepositions, prepositions-conjunctions (words that can serve either function), and interjections. The following are examples:

Conjunctions
ĉar 'because'   *kvankam* 'although'
ke 'that'   *se* 'if'
ol 'than'   *kvazaŭ* 'as if, as though'

Prepositions
en 'in, into'   *sur* 'on'   *apud* 'near'
ĉirkaŭ 'around'   *ĉe* 'at'   *super* 'above'
antaŭ 'before'   *kontraŭ* 'against'   *al* 'to'
sub 'under'   *post* 'after'   *de* 'of, from, by'
el 'out of'   *jen* 'here is/are'   *laŭ* 'according to'
ekster 'outside'   *pro* 'because of'   *anstataŭ* 'instead of'
inter 'among, between' *por* 'for'   *malgraŭ* 'despite'
tra 'through'   *per* 'by means of'   *kun* 'with'
trans 'across'   *pri* 'about, concerning'   *sen* 'without'
krom 'except'   *preter* 'beyond'   *po* 'at the rate of'
da 'of' (quantities) *je* indefinite preposition (see above)

Prepositions/Conjunctions
dum 'while'   *ĝis* 'until, as far as'

Interjections
ve! 'alas!'   *bis!* 'encore!'

nu! 'oh well, now'   *hej!* 'heh, eh'
ho! 'oh'   *halt!* 'stop!'
fi! 'shame! ugh!'

Note: The class indicator *-e* allows us to transform prepositions into adverbs and underived adverbs into derived (e.g., *ne* → *nee*; *pli* → *plie*; *jus* → *juse*). This practice is so common that synonymous adverbs tend to multiply (*nun/nune, tuj/tuje, jen/jene,* etc.), and synonymous pairs emerge (with slightly different nuances), for example: *sub la tablo/sube de la tablo; en la domo/ene de la domo.*

Combination of Lexical Morphemes

Lexical Morphemes and Characterizers. Theoretically, all morphemes can be combined with one or more characterizer, but in practice, and for purely semantic reasons, some morphemes never are. Morphemes that are never combined with characterizers include the characterizers themselves, verbal inflections, and correlatives of the *-iu, -ia,* and *-io* series. The following observations do not apply to characterizers.

Combination of Lexemes (L + L . . .). Esperanto makes abundant use of the process of compounding, as in the following examples:

okulvitroj eye-glasses = 'spectacles'
celtrafa goal-reaching = 'effective'
anasiri duck-go = 'waddle'
akvoplena water-full = 'full of water'
sammaniere same-manner-ly = 'in the same manner, in the same way'
dekunu ten-one = 'eleven'

Two particularly interesting applications of this process can be noted. The first, reduplication, is uncommon but very expressive:

fojfoje 'from time to time'
plenplena 'very full, full to overflowing'
ruĝruĝa suno 'very red sun'
tuttuta homo 'complete person, a real human being'

The second, very common application is the combination of the verb with its complement:

manpremi iun 'to shake someone's hand'
luktakiri ion to struggle-acquire something = 'to acquire something through a struggle, to seize something'
mortbati iun to death-strike someone = 'to strike someone dead, to beat someone to death'

Combination of Lexical Morphemes (M + M . . .). We have already seen some examples. The following are typical:

> *arigi (ar-ig-i)* 'to assemble'
> *iomete (iom-et-e)* 'somewhat, a little bit'
> *neniigi (neni-ig-i)* 'to nullify, annihilate'
> *aĉulino (aĉ-ul-in-o)* 'a bad woman, a contemptible woman'
> *redisiĝinte (re-dis-iĝ-int-e)* 'having separated again'

Combination of Lexemes and Grammatical Morphemes. There are more examples of this type of combination than of any other because of the productivity of derivations and because the feminine is indicated by a grammatical morpheme. In addition to the simple combination (L + M) of *vir-in-o* 'woman', such complex combinations as the following can be found:

> L + M + M: *vir-in-et-o* 'little woman'
> L + M + M + M: *blond-ul-in-et-o* 'little blonde'
> L + L + M: *man-labor-aĵ-o* 'object made by hand'
> L + L + . . . M + M: *man-labor-ist-in-o* 'female manual worker'

Combination of Grammatical Morphemes and Lexemes (M . . . + L). We can distinguish two varieties. The first is the combination of prefix and lexeme. Of all the derivational prefixes used, the prefix *mal-* is the most original and economical, since it is used to form all opposites: *juna* 'young' *maljuna* 'old', *varma* 'warm' *malvarma* 'cold', and so on. It provides a degree of schematization not found in the more naturalistic (and hence more difficult to memorize) planned languages. Our second category consists of grammatical morphemes other than derivations. All categories of grammatical morphemes can be combined with lexemes, as in the following examples:

> *ĉi-vespere* 'this evening, on this evening'
> *ĉiopova* 'all-powerful, capable of everything'
> *ekamo* 'falling in love, beginning of love'
> *fiago* 'immoral act'

nerevena 'not coming back'
u-modo 'imperative mood'
as-tempo 'present tense'

Prepositions play a particularly important role in word building, and two types of prepositional compounds exist: (1) in which the compound form is a word with a new meaning (*labori* 'work' *kunlabori* 'collaborate', *porti* 'carry' *elporti* 'endure', *iri* 'go' *eniri* 'enter'), and (2) in which the compound does not take on a new meaning but rather results in an adverbial phrase of manner (*poresperanta agado* = *agado por Esperanto* 'action on behalf of Esperanto'; *enurba trafiko* = *trafiko en la urbo* 'urban traffic'; *dummilite* = *dum milito* 'during wartime'). The first type of prepositional compound is semantic, the second grammatical.

Mixed Combinations (M . . . + L + M . . .). Examples of this variety are common:

pligrandigi (*pli-grand-ig-i*) 'to make larger'
maljunulo (*mal-jun-ul-o*) 'old person'
malpligrandigi (*mal-pli-grand-ig-i*) 'to make smaller'
enterigo (*en-ter-ig-o*) 'burial'
malsanulejo (*mal-san-ul-ej-o*) 'hospital'
neprizorgemulo (*ne-pri-zorg-em-ul-o*) 'ne'er-do-well, careless or neglectful person'
seniluziigi (*sen-iluzi-ig-i*) 'to disillusion'

We also occasionally find other combinations, for example:

L . . . + M . . . + L: *francdevena* (*franc-de-ven-a*) 'of French origin'
L + M + L + M: *sonelvokiveco* (*son-el-vok-iv-ec-o*) 'power to evoke sounds'

THE SENTENCE

Elements of the Utterance

The utterance in its simplest form can be reduced to a verbal grammatical morpheme (e.g., *ek!* 'let us begin!') or a verb form (lexeme + verbal inflection) that has no subject: *diru* 'tell' (imperative); *pluvas* 'it is raining'; *sufiĉas* 'that's enough'; *tagiĝas* 'it's daybreak'.

The nucleus of the utterance (predicate) is a verb form, to which the various other constituents relate according to their various functions. These functions are indicated, except in the underived adverbs, through a function indicator in the accusative-illative-allative. In the nominative case, this indicator merges with the characterizer (*-o, -a, -e*). The other cases, equally devoid of inflection, are indicated not by final inflections but by introductory morphemes (i.e., prepositions). Because prepositions operate as function indicators and hence as characterizers, we can regard all prepositional phrases as examples of prepositional cases.

Internal Agreement

Noun and adjective agree in number and case (*divers-a-j gazet-o-j; infan-a-n fantazi-o-n*). Internal agreement distinguishes the descriptive function (*mi trovis tiun frukton bongustan,* 'I found that good-tasting fruit') from the attributive (*mi trovis tiun frukton bongusta* 'I found that fruit [to be] good tasting'). When the subject is understood or takes the form of an infinitive or proposition (or clause), the attribute is not in *-a* but in *-e* (e.g., *estas logike konkludi . . .* 'it is logical to conclude').[7]

Case

The *-ies* series of correlatives is a form of genitive:

> *ies = de iu* 'of somebody, somebody's'
> *ties = de tiu* 'of that [person], that person's' (cf. German *dessen*)
> *kies = de kiu* 'of whom, whose' (cf. German *wessen*)
> *ĉies = de ĉiu* 'of everybody, everybody's'
> *nenies = de neniu* 'of no one, no one's'

The *n*-case, generally called the accusative, in fact covers several functions in addition to the accusative. It is used for dates (*la unuan de majo* '[on] the first of May') and for measures, in instances where no preposition is used:

Ĝi estas tri metrojn alta (or *ĝi altas tri metrojn*). 'It is three meters high'.
  (Cf. *ĝi estas alta je tri metroj, ĝi altas je tri metroj*.)
Li vivis dudek jarojn. 'He lived twenty years'. (Cf. *li vivis dum dudek jaroj*.)

As far as the locative is concerned, matters are rather more complicated. We use the *n*-case to indicate that an object goes from one place to another (allative), as in *la kato saltas sur la tablon* 'the cat jumps onto the table', but not when this object or thing remains in the same place, as in *la kato kuŝas sur la tablo*. This 'accusative of direction' also serves to remove the ambiguity of certain prepositions of place, notably *en, sur, sub, super, trans, apud,* which have both meanings. It can also be used without a preposition after verbs of motion toward (*mi kuras la lernejon = mi kuras al la lernejo*). Hence the *n*-form takes the place of *al*.

We should also note that adverbs of place ending in *-e* take an *-n* to indicate direction: *paŝi antaŭen* 'to walk forward' is different from *paŝi antaŭe* 'to walk in front'.

The *n*-case also indicates manner: *oni pendigis lin kapon malsupren* 'they [one] hung him head downward' (i.e., *oni pendigis lin kun la kapo malsupre* 'they hung him with his head down [at the bottom]'). Furthermore, in this case it is clear that the addition of the *-n* takes the place of a preposition. This form is always permissible as long as it does not conflict with some other use of the *-n* in such a fashion as to cause confusion. The preposition thus freed can be prefixed to the verb, if it is transitive: *ni diskutos la aferon = ni diskutos pri la afero = ni pridiskutos la aferon* 'we shall discuss the matter'.

Finally, Esperanto has the capacity, though it is rarely used, of using the accusative form after a noun: *la enkondukado en la tuta mondo unu neŭtralan lingvon = la enkondukado en la tuta mondo de unu neŭtrala lingvo* 'the introduction into the whole world of one neutral language'. This usage, although employed by Zamenhof, is unusual in the Indo-European languages and has accordingly become archaic, but it corresponds well with turns of phrase used in Semitic languages. Consider the following passage from Deuteronomy, in its standard Esperanto form and in a literal Esperanto translation from the Hebrew:

> ... *ĉar Dio amas vin kaj plenumas la promeson, kiun li promesis al viaj patroj, Dio savis vin* . . . .

> ... *pro la dia amado vin kaj pro plenumado lia la promesojn, kiujn li promesis al viaj patroj, savis vin Dio* . . . .

... it is because the Lord loves you, and is keeping the oath which he swore to your fathers, that the Lord has brought you out.... [RSV, Deut. 7:8]

The accusative gives Esperanto great clarity and flexibility.[8] Some authors of planned languages see the accusative as a difficulty and accordingly eliminate it from their projects. Although many ethnic languages have preserved an accusative morpheme, the history of many others shows rapid erosion of its use. Yet its expressive and syntactical advantages in Esperanto are considerable. For example, it makes possible the distinction of descriptive from attributive forms (see above). It also facilitates ellipsis: whereas in English we say "He received him as a prince," thereby leaving it unclear whether "as a prince" relates to subject or object, in Esperanto we can differentiate between the two: *li akceptis lin kiel princo* 'he received him as a prince would receive him', *li akceptis lin kiel princon* 'he received him as he would receive a prince'.

We see a similar distinction in the following two sentences in Esperanto, both of which would be translated into English as 'He loved his son, that conqueror':

> *Li amis sian filon, tiu venkinto.*
> *Li amis sian filon, tiun venkinton.*

The accusative provides Esperanto syntax with greater flexibility and freedom. Indicated by a final morpheme, the grammatical object can occupy any position in the sentence, which can in turn be adapted to virtually any syntactical model.[9] This quality makes Esperanto extraordinarily suitable for translation because it can often express the various syntactic characteristics of ethnic languages. In conclusion, then, we can summarize case in Esperanto as follows:

Subjective case	no inflection
Objective case	ending in -*n* (final inflection)
Prepositional case	preposition (beginning inflection)
Mixed case	preposition plus final -*n*

The Structural Characterizers -a *and* -e

Adjectival or adverbial phrases beginning with a preposition can be transformed into compound adjectives and adverbs by means of the characterizers -a and -e. For example, the sentence *la trafiko per tera vojo duobliĝas dum la somero en la lando* 'traffic on land routes doubles during the summer in the country [nation]' can be rendered as *la tervoja trafiko duobliĝas enlande dumsomere*. The sentence can be expressed still more concisely: *duobliĝas enlande la dumsomera tervoja trafiko*.

Combined Substitutes

For economy of expression, certain groups of words can be replaced by a single word. This is one of the aims of the correlatives:

> *ies libro = la libro de iu* 'the book of someone'
> *neniel sukcesi = sukcesi per neniu maniero* 'to succeed in no way'
> *neniom kolera = tute ne kolera* 'not at all angry, to no degree angry'

Many adverbs in -e can thus be substituted for adverbial phrases using the procedure shown in the previous paragraph:

> *la lastan fojon = lastfoje* 'the last time'
> *en ia grado = iagrade* 'to some degree'
> *en tiu kazo = tiukaze* 'in that case'

We have already had occasion to allude to this tendency in our discussion of particles.

Compound Tenses

In addition to the simple tenses formed by verbal inflections and usable for all normal purposes, compound tenses can be formed by the verb *esti* plus participles. Participles are verbal adjectives showing either that the subject is the agent (active voice) or that the subject is acted upon (passive voice). In the active voice the compound forms provide greater precision with respect to time, on which the simple forms sometimes give insufficient clarity. In the passive there are no simple forms and hence compound forms must be used.

TABLE 8
Compound Tenses.

Auxiliary	Active	Passive
estas *estis* *estos* *estus* *estu* *esti*	*-anta(j)*: -ing *-inta(j)*: having . . . -ed *-onta(j)*: being about to	*-ata(j)*: being . . . -ed *-ita(j)*: having been . . . -ed *-ota(j)*: being about to be . . . -ed

The following examples show the use of compound tenses:

> *esti skribanta* 'to be writing'
> *mi estas skribinta* I am having-written = 'I have written'
> *mi estis skribinta* I have-been having-written = 'I had written'
> *mi estas skribonta* 'I am about to write'
> *la letero estis skribata* 'the letter was being written'
> *la letero estis skribita* 'the letter was (has been) written'

Aspect

Aspect in Esperanto is as much a matter of nouns as of verbs. *Sano* 'health', *sanigi* 'to cure', and *saniga* 'curative' are all formed from a single Esperanto lexeme, although in other languages different lexemes may be required (French has different lexemes for all three: *santé*, *guérir*, *curatif*, respectively). On many occasions there exists no ethnic-language lexical equivalent at all, and we are obliged to use circumlocution of some kind.

From a syntactic point of view, the aspectual prefixes and suffixes lend conciseness and elegance to the utterance. In the following example two combined aspects equal an entire proposition:

*Mi havas celon, kiun mi povos atingi nur **ekriĉiĝinte**.*
'I have a goal which I shall be able to reach only **when I have begun to become rich**'.

Transitivity

Transitivity is not limited to verbs in Esperanto: nouns, adjectives, and adverbs can also take a transitive construction. Thus, in addition to the schema verb + direct object (e.g., *enkonduki Esperanton* 'to introduce Esperanto'), we find:

noun + direct object: *enkonduko Esperanton = enkonduko de Esperanto* 'introduction of Esperanto' (this is rare; see above)

adjective + direct object: *inda atenton = inda je atento* 'worthy of attention'

adverb + direct object: *rilate la aferon = en rilato al la afero* 'in relation to the matter, concerning the matter'

A transitive lexeme is made intransitive by adding the suffix *-iĝ*, as in the following pairs:

> *fini* 'to finish' (trans.) (*mi finas la libron* 'I finish the book')
> *finiĝi* 'to finish' (intrans.) (*la libro finiĝas* 'the book ends')
> *fino* 'end' (*la fino de la libro* 'the end of the book')
> *finiĝo* 'end' (*la finiĝo de la pluvo* 'the end[ing] of the rain')
> *komenci* 'to begin' (trans.)
> *komenciĝi* 'to begin' (intrans.)

An intransitive lexeme is made transitive by adding the suffix *-ig*, as follows:

ĉesi 'to stop' (intrans.) *la pluvo ĉesas* 'the rain stops'
ĉesigi 'to stop' (trans.) *ŝi ĉesigas la laboron* 'she stops (the) work'
ĉeso 'the action of ceasing' *la ĉeso de la pluvo* 'the stopping of the rain'
ĉesigo 'the action of stopping' *la ĉesigo de la laboro* 'the stopping of the work'
daŭri 'to continue' (intrans.) *la laboro daŭris* 'the work continued'
daŭrigi 'to continue' (trans.) *ŝi daŭrigis la laboron* 'she continued [made-to-continue] the work'

Confusion can arise from the fact that transitivity is not always indicated by a separate morpheme. Hence *-ig* and *-iĝ* are often used superfluously in spoken language, that is to say in the form of theoretically useless—but in practice clarifying—redundancies, and one occasionally meets *finigi* instead of *fini*, or *ĉesiĝi* instead of *ĉesi*. Although purists are unwilling to accept such redundancies, they are nonetheless a common and generally healthy phenomenon in many languages and may even be recommended when they improve clarity and comprehensibility.

The Reflexive Possessive

The adjective and pronoun *sia*, derived from the pronoun *si* 'him/her/it-self', refers back to the subject of the proposition in which it is found. Consider the following:

La frato diras al sia fratino ...
'The brother says to his [the brother's] sister ...
... ke ilia patro
... that their father [*sia* is not used with a subject]
... petas ŝin legi sian libron
... asks her to read her book [i.e., that book belonging to the antecedent of *read*]
... pensante pri sia ekzameno
... thinking about (keeping in mind) [a participial adverb referring back to the antecedent of *read*] her [i.e., that belonging to the antecedent of *thinking about*] examination'.

Negatives and Interrogatives

The negative is formed by the particle *ne*:

Esperanto	English	French
mi ne dormas	I do **not** sleep	*je **ne** dors **pas***
nemulte	**not** much	***pas** beaucoup*
nefera	**non**ferrous	***non**ferreux*
nekredebla	**in**credible	***in**croyable*
nesana	**un**healthy	***mal**sain*

Questions are formed with the particle *ĉu*, except when a question is introduced by one of the correlatives: *ĉu vi venas?* but *de kie vi venas?* The particle *ĉu* can also be used as a subordinating conjunction: *mi ne scias, ĉu li venas* 'I do not know whether he is coming'. Finally, it can serve as a coordinating conjunction: *ĉu por vivo, ĉu por morto* 'whether for life or for death'.

Word Order

The existence of the accusative and the various inflectional devices in Esperanto allows for great flexibility in word order: a phrase such as *la de vi montrita vojo* 'the by-you-shown way' is as acceptable as the more English-sounding *la vojo montrita de vi* 'the way shown by you'. The phrase 'the only foundation, required for all Esperantists once and for all' may be rendered as *la sola fundamento, deviga por ĉiuj esperantistoj unu fojon por ĉiam* or equally well as *la sola, unu fojon por ĉiam deviga por ĉiu esperantisto fundamento.*

Epithets are normally placed before the noun, subjects before the verb, complements after the verb, adverbs in front of the word they qualify. Syntactically, then, Esperanto belongs to the most frequent language type, namely the so-called SVO type (subject-verb-object), to which the Romance, Germanic, and Slavic languages belong. These languages automatically provided a syntactical model to the first Esperantists, but no rules on this matter appear among the well-known Sixteen Rules, which implies that the first students of Esperanto were obliged to conform to the usage prevalent in their own languages. Today, it is perfectly reasonable to argue that Esperanto syntax allows Japanese speakers to render 'the dog saw the cat' as *la hundo la katon vidis* or Arabic speakers to say *vidis la hundo la katon*, just as they would in their own languages, as long as rules of clarity and comprehensibility are observed.

Subordination

Subordinate clauses linked to the predicate can be classified as subject propositions, object propositions, or adverbial propositions, depending on the circumstances:

Nominative (-o): *Estas bone ke li revenis. = Lia reveno estas bona.* 'It is good that he has come back'.
Accusative (-on): *Ni esperu, ke li revenos. = Ni esperu lian revenon.* 'Let us hope that he will return'.
Adverbial: *Mi ĝojas, ĉar li revenis. = Mi ĝojas pro lia reveno.* 'I am glad he has returned'.

Subordinate clauses linked to an element in the utterance other than the predicate may be introduced by subordinating conjunctions, or may appear as relatives, introduced by one of the correlatives, as in the following examples:

Mi ne komprenas (tion), kion vi diras. 'I do not understand what you are saying'.
Li estas (tiel) granda, kiel vi. 'He is as big as you'.
Li alvenis (tiam), kiam ni foriris. 'He arrived when we left'.

The use of mood and tense indicators depends on the meaning of the conjunction or correlative used. Thus, the subjunctive is used after *por ke* 'so that', but the indicative after *kvankam* 'although'. After *se*, the conditional indicates hypothesis, the indicative implies possibility or probability, and the volitive (the *u*-mood) obligation:

> *Se mi povus, mi venus.* 'If I could, I would come'
> *Se mi povos, mi venos.* 'If I can, I will come'
> *Se ni komparu lin kun. . . .* 'If we must compare him with . . .'

TOWARD A GRAMMATICAL DESCRIPTION BASED ON ZAMENHOF'S PRINCIPLES[10]

Intrasyntagmatic and Intersyntagmatic Rules

Zamenhof acknowledged that he sought to present his language in terms as didactically appropriate as possible to the customary usage of educated Europeans. Given his theory of language, he might well have developed a revolutionary grammar of the kind that was to appear seventy years later in and about the ethnic languages. The didactic value of these newer grammars is not always clear, and Esperanto continues to need teachers rather than theorists. However, the originality of Zamenhof's theory allows us to imagine a grammar based on its innovations as a means of examining the surface and latent structures of the language.

Consider the following sentence: *La patro de la infanoj laboras multe* 'The father of the children works a lot'. If we apply a generative analysis to it, we see that the sentence consists of syntagms (strings of constituents) which, as a group, have a single function:

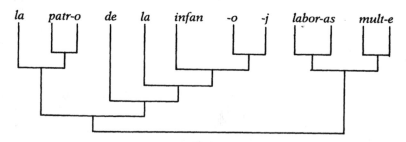

The syntagms are as follows:

subjective   predicative

patro	*infano*	
	infanoj	
la patro	*la infanoj*	
	de la infanoj	*laboras multe*

The constituents of these syntagms are related to one another through two types of rules, intrasyntagmatic and intersyntagmatic. The intrasyntagmatic rules are those that operate within the syntagm. For example, *patro* implies a rule about the position of *patr-* and *-o*; *la patro* implies a further rule about the position of *la*; *de la infanoj* implies rules about the position of *-j*, *-o*, *infan-*, *la*, and *de*.

     The intersyntagmatic rules are those describing the position of the various syntagms in relation to one another. For example *de la infanoj* may appear either to the right or to the left of *la patro*, *la patro de la infanoj* can appear to right or left of *laboras multe*, *multe* can appear before or after *laboras* or before *la patro de la infanoj*, but not within *la patro de la infanoj*.

     The intrasyntagmatic rules can be summarized as follows:

1. The monemes (grammatical morphemes) *-as*, *-is*, *-os*, *-us*, *-u*, *-i*, *-n* indicate the end of a syntagm.
2. The moneme *-j* appears after the monemes *-o*, *-a*, *-ia*, *-iu*, but before *-n*. Its intrasyntagmatic position is either at the end or before the end when the ending is *-n*.
3. The moneme *-a* normally does not mark the end of a syntagm; it can appear before *-n*, *-j*, and *-jn*.
4. The moneme *-o* appears at the end of a syntagm or before *-n*, *-j*, *-jn*.
5. The moneme *-e* indicates the end of a syntagm except when the ending is *-n*.
6. Numbers and particles (articles, interrogatives and negatives, conjunctions, prepositions, subordinating conjunctions) mark the beginning of a syntagm.
7. A few monemes can play the role of syntagms (e.g., pronouns).
8. Lexemes may mark the beginning but not the end of a syntagm. (This rule does not apply to poetry.)

The intersyntagmatic rules are of two kinds: positional and relational. Positional rules prescribe the position of a syntagm in a larger structure. For example, we can say either *bela domo* or *domo bela*. There is, then, a rule stipulating that *bela* can appear either before or after *domo*. Another rule defines the cases in which a preposition can appear before or after the verb; so we know that *iri en domon* is the same as *eniri domon*.

The relational rules clarify the grammatical relations between the syntagms regardless of their position. They are of two types: first, rectional (governing) rules prescribe the compulsory use of certain monemes in relation to others: *obei **iun**, obei al **iu**, por ke **ili povu**, ni **esperantistoj**, **iri** en domo, **iri** en **domon***; second, congruent rules prescribe the repetition of certain monemes in given positions: *bela**j** libro**j**, bela**n** libro**n***; *se mi estu**s** riĉa, mi aĉetu**s** domon.*

Transformational Rules

The above rules concern the surface structure of the language. The speaker who applies them properly will use the language correctly. But for the linguist they are insufficient to describe all the operations that take place when the language is used. If we consider the sentences *li eniras la domon* and *li iras en la domon*, we can readily assert that the two have different surface structures. Yet they have the same meaning. Accordingly, we say that their deep structure is the same. Surface structure is concerned with the order and sequence of constituents; deep structure is an abstraction in the mind of the speaker. We are aware of the deep structure only because we can change the surface structure without changing the meaning. This shows that the two sentences quoted above repose on a common structure that we shall not find in the dictionary. Transformational rules, then, are processes that transform the abstract mental conception into concrete monemes (morphemes), syntagms, and propositions. They are expressed through pairs or chains of equivalents:

> *mi miras pro lia scio*   = *lia scio mirigas min*
> 'I am amazed at his knowledge'   'his knowledge amazes me'
>   or
> *mi amas vin* = *vin mi amas* = *amas vi min* = *amas vin mi* ...

Important transformational rules apply to many languages. Coordination, subordination, and apposition, for example, are almost universal. Many other transformations are entirely specific to certain languages and serve as a means of highlighting the uniqueness of the language in question. We need only review the following list to understand that the uniqueness of Esperanto lies in its typical transformations:

1. *estas + -a*	is transformed to	*as*-syntagm
estas ruĝa	→	*ruĝas*
2. preposition	is transformed to	*-n*
veturi al Parizo	→	*veturi Parizon*
malsani pro gripo	→	*malsani gripon*
3. *o*-syntagm + *-n*	is transformed to	*e*-syntagm + *-n*
iri hejmon	→	*iri hejmen*
4. *o*-syntagm + predicate	is transformed to	*i*-syntagm + predicate
promeno estas plezuro	→	*promeni estas plezuro*
5. *o*-syntagm + *-n*	is transformed to	*e*-syntagm
ĉiun tagon	→	*ĉiutage*
6. preposition + *o*-syntagm	is transformed to	preposition + *e*-syntagm
sen intenco	→	*senintence*
7. preposition + *o*-syntagm	is transformed to	*e*-syntagm
kun plezuro	→	*plezure*

These rules show that Esperanto is clearly distinguishable from the Indo-European languages and particularly the Romance languages, the very languages to which it owes its original appearance. If we apply our first transformation, above, to verbal periphrasis, we realize that Esperanto does not have to conform to French or English usage, but can be expressed in its own terms—saying, for example, *mi devintus* instead of *mi estus devinta*. Transformation 4 makes clear that the unusual *ni klopodas pri la enkonduko Esperanton en la mondo* 'we are trying for the introduction of Esperanto in the world' (a form used by Zamenhof nonetheless) is entirely justifiable, as is the use of the *i*-syntagm after all prepositions.

Furthermore, these rules encourage grammarians to judge Esperanto usage on its own terms, instead of trying to make it conform to modes of expression in other languages. The conclusions could be, or are in danger of being, surprising. There is, for example, no theoretical reason for declaring the following sentences incorrect:

Mi frapitis martelon de atakanto. = *Mi estis frapita per martelo de atakanto.* 'I was hit with a hammer by an attacker'.

Mi elveturas Svision Francien. = *Mi veturas el Svisio al Francio.* 'I travel out of Switzerland toward France'.

Li nomotas ministro por savo la landon. = *Li estas nomota ministro por savi la landon.* 'He is about to be named minister to save the country'.

This analysis shows just how revolutionary Esperanto is, even for the Esperantists.

Chapter 4

Expression

TRENDS IN THE EVOLUTION OF ESPERANTO

Zamenhof encouraged the Esperantists to make their opinions on the language known, and little by little the criticisms surfaced. From the beginning, he had declared himself willing to introduce extensive reforms, but after the general consultation of 1894 and the decision of the Boulogne congress on the "untouchability" of the *Fundamento*, it was difficult to turn back. Nevertheless, in 1907, alarmed at the emerging intrigues of a few schismatics, Zamenhof once again made proposals for changes that would not antagonize the mainstream conservatism of his followers and would simplify the language still further: diacritical marks on consonants were to be replaced by an *h* after the consonant in question, *ĥ* was to be suppressed in favor of *k*, the adverbial ending *-aŭ* was to be assimilated into the ending *-e*, the accusative would no longer be compulsory, descriptive adjectives could remain unmodified, in the names of countries the derivational morpheme -*i*- would be used in place of -*uj*- (*Francujo* would become *Francio*, *Britujo* would become *Britio*), four new suffixes and three prepositions would be added, and a few changes would be made in the lexicon (*et* instead of *kaj*).

These proposals answer most of the objections raised against Esperanto then and since. Zamenhof knew their value, since in 1894 he himself had suggested, without success, that the accusative be dropped and adjectives be made invariant. These reforms would certainly have simplified the language. Furthermore, they were very much in conformity with the evolution of many ethnic languages, such as Latin, English, Arabic, and so on. However, Esperanto had shown itself to be an effective means of communication from the beginning, and its users had rapidly grown used to the grammar as it was. Literature had begun. Translations were appearing in large numbers. The linguistic conservatism of Esperanto's users was based in part on the success of the language: they were fully aware that the language constituted an integrated whole made up of interdependent and indivisible elements with their own unity, originality, and genius; and finally their experience told them that Esperanto was already sufficiently viable to serve a noble human purpose, compared to which linguistic disputes seemed a purely academic and unimportant matter.

This conservatism suggests that there are two ways of looking at what happened later. When, in 1908, the would-be reformers left the Esperanto movement to create Ido (that is, Esperanto reformed by Louis Couturat and Louis de Beaufront in accordance with their own linguistic principles), they set off in a quite different direction. Consciously or unconsciously, they had no intention of limiting themselves to the improvement of a few grammatical or lexical points: their "improvements" in fact changed the entire appearance of Esperanto and in no way accorded with its spirit. The forty or more projects derived from Esperanto and Ido reflect a tendency to greater naturalism in imitation of the Romance languages. Paradoxically, their authors criticized Esperanto for its excessive rationality and then for subjective and aesthetic reasons proceeded to regress to a lower level of clarity and internationality. In parallel with this essentially psychological disagreement, there also emerged a political conflict concerning the role and aims of an international language. Neither the Idists nor the Esperantists seemed willing to try to come to an agreement. Very possibly the discussions between them in the period from 1907 to 1925 could have reached a technical compromise, were it not for this more or less conscious preexisting ideological conflict.

After 1908 Esperanto entered a phase of internal development in the context of the *Fundamento*. From this point on, it became the task of the Esperanto Academy to inspire respect for the fundamental principles of the language and to monitor its development. It accepted a few of the changes proposed in 1907: *ĥ* is not used in neologisms; *-uj-* is permitted but not required in the names of trees and countries (*pomujo = pomarbo*; *Anglujo = Anglio*); new derivatives have been added to the original list (*produkt-iv-a, najl-iz-i, semicirkla, retroiri*); a few naturalistic neologisms have been introduced to avoid confusion or limit the meaning of certain compounds (e.g., *heĝo = dornbarilo, kanono = pafilego, oblikva = malrekta, armeo = militistaro*) or when the original compound is too long or impractical in modern use (*maldekstra = liva*). Specific national terms have come into Esperanto essentially without change (*samovaro, samurajo*), though on the other hand certain international words like *agrikulturo* and *aeronaŭtiko* have taken the place of *kampokultivado* 'field cultivation' and *aerveturado* 'air travel'. Overall, the language has adapted well to the enormous changes that have overtaken the world since 1887 without modifying its basic structure. More dangerous than the rival language projects published during this period have been the massive scientific, technical, and economic developments that have swept through society between then and now. Also the growing number of users of Esperanto across the world, with their various linguistic traditions, has subjected the structural cohesion of the language to considerable strain, but in this respect as well Esperanto has proven to be flexible, plastic, and, in a word, international. These decisive tests have brought it successfully from the experimental stage to its current self-sustaining condition. Exploiting the potential contained in the *Fundamento*, modern usage is not limited to the usage employed by Zamenhof. On his original foundation new structures have been built—structures that would certainly collapse without the Boulogne agreements to support them, but that differ from what was then current. Like any other linguistic system, Esperanto now functions independently, in accordance with its own rules and not on the basis of decisions by outside agencies. Zamenhof created a project, but the Esperanto community has made it a language—a phenomenon unique in the history of language.

EXPRESSIVE RESOURCES

As we have noted, the evolution of Esperanto is determined by collective linguistic usage and practice. The use of Esperanto in the various sciences has enriched the vocabulary with an abundance of scientific terms, generally adaptations of words of international currency, in accordance with Zamenhof's fifteenth rule (see chap. 3). A growing and constantly updated lexicon is at the disposal of researchers in almost every branch of learning. As early as 1910 the *Enyclopedic Glossary of Esperanto* (*Enciklopedia vortareto Esperanta*) of Charles Verax brought together more than 12,000 words from all branches of science, and by 1914 there were about fifteen specialized scientific publications in circulation. Today there are over 160 specialized dictionaries in fifty or more fields, including cybernetics, mathematics, informatics, law, medicine, theology, chemistry, meteorology, gastronomy, and so on. Of these, thirty-three have between 75 and 300 pages, five have more than 300 pages, and the others are smaller. Taken together, they constitute a collection that relatively few languages could equal. This vocabulary has been elaborated and developed by learned societies (which we shall discuss below), in their meetings, correspondence, and publications. Several of the publications reach a sophisticated technical level, such as the journals *Scienca revuo* and *Biblia revuo*, the papers of the Summer University Courses, the publications of the Institute for Pedagogical Cybernetics (FEoLL), the series of documents published by the Center for Research and Documentation on World Language Problems (in Esperanto CED, in English CRD), a number of doctoral dissertations, and so on.[1]

Esperanto's suitability as a means of scientific communication has engaged the attention of numerous scholars. As early as 1924, forty-two members of the French Academy of Sciences, among them such eminent figures as de Broglie, Cotton, Lumière, Painlevé, Perrin, Branly, and Charcot, declared themselves "convinced that the adoption of the auxiliary language Esperanto in international relations would have consequences of immense import for the progress and application of the sciences." They expressed the desire that this language, "a masterpiece of logic and simplicity," should be introduced into the teaching of science, instituted as the official language of international conferences, and used in scientific publications and exchanges. Similar opinions were regularly expressed in other countries as well.[2]

The use of Esperanto as a literary and artistic language raises problems more complex in nature. Scientists may be said to construct their own language, but they do not use it to express emotional nuances or for aesthetic effect. It is significant that in the first Esperanto booklet of 1887 Zamenhof published three poems and that one third of the *Fundamenta krestomatio* is devoted to original and translated poetry. From the beginning, Esperantists have been concerned with the aesthetic aspects and values of their language. They have been well aware of the fact that criteria of beauty in a planned language may be different from those in ethnic languages, but they will be linguistically derived nonetheless. Esperanto's original literature has served as a device for the elaboration and testing of the aesthetic rules implicit in the structure and principles of the language. In Esperanto, an expression or utterance is beautiful insofar as it coincides with the unique spirit of the language, be it prosodic, morphological, or syntactical.

The flexibility and variety of compounds in Esperanto allows for remarkable lexical economy (e.g., *iri/supreniri/mal-supreniri* 'to go/to go upward/to go downward'), but this educational and practical advantage has its negative aspect for literary expression, since it results in the frequent repetition of roots and the creation of polysyllabic words. Accordingly, "naturalisms" like *ascendi* and *descendi*, or *olda* (for *maljuna* 'old') have entered the language, creating parallel lists of synonyms by which to express particular nuances or achieve specific effects. Just as in English we find Germanic terms alternating with terms from Latin or French, so in Esperanto simple forms parallel the compound ones:

> *elpensi* 'to think out' = *inventi* 'to invent'
> *vagonaro* 'railroad car group' = *trajno* 'train'
> *flugilo* 'means of flying' = *alo* 'wing'
> *vinbero* 'wine berry' = *uvo* 'grape'

This important concession to naturalism shows that the literary aesthetic continues to depend in some measure on classical Western criteria and does not easily accord with too rigid a schematism. But this naturalized vocabulary remains limited in large measure to literary use, particularly poetry, and it would be unjustified to conclude that there exists in Esperanto a general tendency to replace compounds and derivations with naturalistic synonyms. In everyday usage the latter are infrequent (and even in poetry they are not exclusively used), and it is estimated that no more than a sixth of the compound words contained in the *Fundamento* have their naturalistic equivalents. This being so, there is no risk that they will upset the internal lexical balance of the language.

If too zealous an application of schematism may sometimes seem too heavy or crudely analytical, it nevertheless provides a conciseness and density of expression that many ethnic languages cannot match because they are obliged to use complex circumlocutions to express the same meaning. For example, on the model of *samlandano* ('same-country-member' = 'compatriot'), Esperanto has constructed such terms as *samideano (ideo)* and *samklasano (klaso)*, and in parallel with *samaĝulo* (same-age-person) we have such words as *samprofesiulo (profesio)*. Esperanto expresses, through a single compact combination, the idea of putting something into the dictionary or removing it (*envortarigi/elvortarigi*) or putting somebody or something to bed (*enlitigi*), or on a table (*surtabligi*), or under water (*subakvigi*). Such words as *tranokti, envagoniĝi, ekzameniĝi, enposteniĝi, emeritiĝi* must be translated in many languages by periphrases and circumlocutions, though it is important to note that these circumlocutions can be rendered into perfectly correct Esperanto as well:

tranokti = *pasigi la nokton* 'to pass the night, to stay overnight'
envagoniĝi = *eniri en vagonon* 'to get into the railroad car, to entrain'
ekzameniĝi = *fari ekzamenon* 'to take an examination, to be examined'
enposteniĝi = *akcepti postenon* 'to enter employment, to be installed'
emeritiĝi = *fariĝi emerito* 'to enter retirement, to retire'

There are numerous examples of such double or multiple possibilities. We can say equally correctly *bluokula knabo* 'blue-eyed boy' and *knabo kun bluaj okuloj* 'boy with blue eyes', *vivo en urbo* 'life in a city' and *enurba vivo* 'city life', *dum la periodo post la milito* 'during the period after the war' and *dum la postmilita periodo* 'during the postwar period'—but if these Esperanto phrases all have their acceptable equivalents in English, many others do not. This diversity of options enriches the powers of expression and accordingly facilitates stylistic effect.

There are other advantages too. The sentence *li sendas paketojn per la poŝto trans la limojn* 'he sends packages by mail across the frontiers' is modeled on French, English, and German syntax. Accordingly, we can assert that it presents a certain measure of internationality. But if we look at the same sentence dressed differently—*Li sendas paketojn perpoŝte translimen*—we note that an Esperantist understands it equally clearly, but that a speaker of French, English, or German cannot render it word by word in his or her own language because the surface structure has changed significantly: the prepositional syntagms have been transformed into adverbs and the essentially analytic structure has become more synthetic. So we can conclude that Esperanto is suitable for all speakers, whether their native languages are analytic or synthetic. We reached a similar conclusion in chapter 3 in our observations on the *n*-case and its use in the translation of Semitic forms. Thus Esperanto can assimilate to itself more structures than any individual ethnic language. In this adaptability lies its true internationality. Although it is not limitless, it far exceeds what is possible in other languages, making Esperanto an international language in the fullest sense.

The schematic nature of word building in Esperanto brings many advantages in the expression of nuances of ideas and feelings. The general concept *kulturo* is distinguished from *kulturiteco*, the quality of a cultured person; *vivo* is more general than *vivanteco*, the state of being alive; *imitebla* and *imitinda* express the difference between the possibility and the desirability of imitation; *farendaĵo* is not the same as *farotaĵo* or *farindaĵo* (something that must be done, that will be done, and that is worth doing, respectively). Prefixes enlarge expressive capability with maximum lexemic economy: one *ellasas* ('lets out') a prisoner from a jail, *forlasas* ('leaves behind') a place or a person, *delasas* ('lets down', 'lowers') curtains (which one can *kuntiri* 'pull together' or *distiri* 'pull apart'). One *prenas* ('takes') a book from the table, but a verb *alprenas* an ending, a bus *enprenas* passengers, a policeman *deprenas* your documents from you and sometimes, alas, *forprenas* them, even if you *kunprenis* only a bottle of soda. This construction allows us to describe movement through the verb and direction through a prefixed preposition: **enkuri, forflugi, subrampi,** and so on.

The abundant possibilities for the combination of morphemes permit great economy in morphology and syntax and allow for greater precision of meaning. By combining lexemes, it is possible to express new concepts using old ones (*lit* + *tuk* = *littuko* '[bed] sheet'), rather than creating a new root, as Romance languages tend to do. The following table shows how seven Esperanto words can do the work of thirteen French words, and almost as many English ones. This economy is a valuable asset in learning and memorizing the language.

Esperanto	English	French
tuko	cloth, sheet	*linge*
naz-tuko (nose)	handkerchief	*mouchoir*
lit-tuko (bed)	[bed] sheet	*drap* [de lit]
kap-tuko (head)	[head] scarf	*fichu*
tablo-tuko (table)	tablecloth	*nappe*
antaŭ-tuko (before)	apron	*tablier*
man-tuko (hand)	towel	*essuie-mains*

The compounds thus formed all have a single meaning, although the French and English equivalents in several cases have more than one meaning, thereby possibly creating confusion for the student. They are also economical with respect to syntax, since the system allows for the linking of verb and complement in a single, tight compound, as in *mansvingi* 'to wave one's hand', *kapjesi* 'to nod one's head affirmatively', *temporaba* 'time consuming', *anasiri* 'to waddle', *korŝira* 'heart rending'. The ability to create compounds of this kind allows for the creation of metaphorical combinations, which are among the most productive of poetic tropes in Esperanto. Thus Kalocsay writes:

*Ne taŭzis la suprajon ankoraŭ **kiso-mevoj**.*
The surface has not yet been ruffled by **the kiss of gulls** (lit. kiss-gulls).[3]

The structure of Esperanto favors adjectival combinations like *ŝia voĉo, orsona, dolĉanĝela* 'her voice, gold-sounding, sweet-angelic', and *e*-syntagms (see chap. 3), which provide extreme density of expression through a simple sentence element, as in the following line by Brendon Clark: *Dio, pro kies ordono la suno turmentas skarlate* 'God, at whose decree the sun torments scarletly'. Such examples show the expressive quality that the language gains from the fact that its lexemes are not tightly governed by grammatical category. In the following haiku the Japanese poet Miyamoto Masao uses lexemes of imprecise grammatical value with an effect all the greater for the imprecision:

> *Marhorizonto*
> *majpluve nun nebulas,*
> *nur mut'—marondo.*
> 'sea-horizon/ like-May-rain now mists/ only muteness—sea-wave'

The beauty of these lines lies largely in the fact that nouns behave like adverbs or verbs and an adjective becomes a noun. We are dealing here not with a poetic convention but with a fundamental characteristic of the language—a characteristic further illustrated in the ability to use grammatical morphemes as lexical units, thereby enriching the vocabulary with a whole series of lexemes derived from essentially grammatical devices: *ano = membro, ajo = objekto, aro = grupo, ejo = loko, eta = malgranda, ege = multe, ene = interne*, and so on. These can be considered as authentic Esperantisms—as can constructions which in a sense move in the opposite direction: *suni, furiozi, fervori, malĉasti, ebli*, and others.

We have already explained how the existence of the accusative and of adjectival agreement expands the flexibility of the syntax by allowing us to invert or transform the word order to highlight a given word:

> *ni sidis sub verda arbo* 'we sat under a green tree'
> *sub verda arbo ni sidis*
> *sub arbo verda sidis ni*
> *ni sub arbo verda sidis*

Zamenhof evokes a leafy romanticism in a slightly different way:

> *sub arbo sub verda ni sidis*

Antoni Grabowski moves article and adjective behind the noun to achieve the following effect:

> *kiel vento la blovanta* 'like wind the blowing'

and a similar separation of normally contiguous sentence elements allows Aymonnier to write *Vi malluman tuŝas arbon* (you a dark touch tree). The following passage from the poem *"Elegie"* (Elegiacally) of Nicolino Rossi illustrates some of the linguistic devices whereby a talented poet can satisfy the most demanding critic:

> *Ventoblov': branĉomov'*
> *dancema.*
> *Ventozum': ora lum'*
> *ekstrema*
> *volvas jen valon en*
> *orfluo*
> *por la vid' gaja rid'*
> *kaj ĝuo.*
> *El tra nub', el tra rub'*
> *ĉiela*
> *ridas nun brila sun'*
> *kaj bela*
> *pentras ĝi per radi'*
> *la valon.*
> *Gaja hen': vokas jen*
> *ĉevalon.*

'Windblowing: branchmoving / dance-wanting. / Windrustle: gold light / extreme [formerly trembling?] / envelops (look!) valley in / goldflow / for seeing happy laughing / and joy.

From through cloud, from through rubble / of sky / laughs now a shining sun / (and beautiful) / paints it with ray / the valley. / A cheerful neighing: calls (hear!) / a horse'.[4]

The poet is able to use such techniques (peculiar to Esperanto) as combining nouns, varying the position of adjectives, reversing subjects, and juxtaposing prepositions to create the particular combination of rhythm, rhyme, and descriptive language that produces the magical quality of this untranslatable poem, whose suggestive density and sensuous quality are more reminiscent of ideograms than of conventional words.

The reader will note how successfully Esperanto uses alliteration and assonance. Despite the fixed accent in Esperanto, elision allows Rossi to alternate amphibrachs (x/x) and cretics (/x/)—that is to say, iambic and trochaic rhythms—a particular characteristic of Esperanto poetry. The purity of Esperanto vowels and the soft flow of its consonants create melodic patterns well suited to the full range of rhetorical techniques.

Such plasticity offers another important benefit: as a language of translation, Esperanto is often able to provide a faithful rendering of the effects used in the original, with the result that Esperanto translations are frequently of higher quality than even the most talented of translations into ethnic languages. Cases in point include the *Kalevala,* the *Divine Comedy,* and various translations of Shakespeare.[5] Not without reason has the literature of Esperanto, original and translated, grown so rapidly within a single century. Aesthetic aspects of the language have played in important role in this process, and we have already seen how the structure of the language offers unique means of expression. Esperanto, then, reveals itself as a language with the potential of translating anything better than other languages can translate it, and also of creating a truly international aesthetic based on its own special character.

Chapter 5

The Literature

We cannot dissociate Esperanto literature from the language itself. Esperanto began, after all, primarily as a written language. Ethnic languages start life as spoken languages and can continue for centuries without ever being written down. Planned languages, on the other hand, are born through the written word, and in large measure their viability depends on their effectiveness as written languages. For seventeen years, Esperanto functioned primarily in written form among widely dispersed users. Although it was also employed in local clubs and regional meetings, the language acquired maturity, realized its latent powers of expression, and established itself as a means of cultural exchange, principally through its written literature. Rather than worrying over details of grammar, Zamenhof preferred, using the *Fundamento* as his grammatical base, to translate as many literary masterpieces as he could: Shakespeare's *Hamlet* (1894), Gogol's *Government Inspector* (1907), Goethe's *Iphigenia auf Tauris* (1908), Schiller's *Die Räuber* (1908), Molière's *Georges Dandin* (1908), Eliza Orzeszkowa's *Marta* (1910), Hans Andersen's fairytales, and the entire Old Testament, as well as a number of less extensive works.[1]

For Zamenhof, translation was a means of refining Esperanto by tackling the difficulties and subtleties of natural languages. Accordingly, he advised translators to choose major works and to hold to the ideal of fidelity to the original, confronting any linguistic obstacle head on. The aim of such activity was first and foremost the enrichment of Esperanto's lexicon. The 912 lexical morphemes of 1887 grew to 2,126 as a result of the series of translations that Zamenhof published in 1907 and 1908, and it is calculated that 1,294 neologisms were introduced by Zamenhof in the same way between 1908 and his death. Waringhien's *Plena ilustrita vortaro* (Complete Illustrated Dictionary), published in 1970, has approximately 15,250 entries (a 1987 supplement adds 850 more, most of them recent coinages). While the entries include numerous technical terms and proper nouns, the majority are new roots, many introduced since the time of Zamenhof, and among them appear the literary doublets mentioned in our previous chapter. Literary scholars look on this increase in the word stock with favor; other voices, however, are raised against a certain affectation inherent in all classicism, and fear that this proliferation of neologisms may weaken Esperanto's simplicity and facility.[2]

The most obvious advantage resulting from the confrontation of Esperanto with the masterworks of national literatures is a gain in expressiveness and a more conscious originality. As Zamenhof foresaw, it is not enough to invent new words: they must also be adapted to the expression of thought and feeling most perfectly represented in great works of literature. To achieve this, Esperanto has been forced to mobilize the resources inherent in its structure and its very nature, and to expand and refine those resources, through contact with life itself, to the point where it can adapt them to all occasions. Originally a means of utilitarian communication, Esperanto has also become a language of art, and this art has found expression in its abundant translated and original literature.[3]

TRANSLATIONS

It has been calculated that at least 10,000 works have been translated into Esperanto, and the number increases by the dozens each year. This production represents activity uninterrupted, except by the world wars, from the beginning of the movement to today. Although uneven in quality, these translations constitute the largest anthology of world culture ever undertaken for popular consumption. Literary works form the largest part of this collection, and almost all major literary figures are represented in the large Esperanto libraries of Vienna, Rotterdam, London, Tokyo, Prague, Lublin, La Chaux-de-Fonds, and elsewhere. Considering that this huge number of translations is addressed to what is still a very limited worldwide public, we can only wonder at the cultural ambition of the Esperantists. It is unlikely that many people would ever be able to read, in the original, works as diverse as *Eugene Onegin*, *Peer Gynt*, *Gösta Berling*, the *Kalevala*, Ihara Saikaku's *Five Courtesans*, the short stories of Lu Hsün, Imre Mádach's *Tragedy of Man*, along with *Faust*, *Othello*, *Oedipus Rex*, and the *Divine Comedy*. It is equally unlikely, even in Western countries, that many people would find translated into their own native languages all the works that have been translated into Esperanto. Esperantists thus have at their disposal a thoroughly representative selection of the literatures of the world. This single fact constitutes, more than all efforts at bilingualism and trilingualism, a genuine step toward the creation of a universal culture.

To introduce their readers to the various literatures, Esperanto publishers offer a wide range of anthologies containing background information on the literatures in question as well as representative texts. Australian, Belgian, Brazilian, Bulgarian, Catalan, Chinese, Croatian, Czech, Danish, Dutch, English, Estonian, French, Hebrew, Italian, Japanese, Korean, Polish, Portuguese, Romanian, Scottish, Swedish, and Swiss anthologies (among others) serve as popular ambassadors for these cultures among Esperanto speakers in other countries. Many of these anthologies present the cultures of less well known countries or national minorities, and not the least of Esperanto's accomplishments is the fact that it has made the general public aware of literature that ordinarily remains the province of specialists.

This accomplishment is not limited to anthologies. The Bulgarian writers Yordan Yovkov, Georgi Karaslavov, Georgi Stamatov, Nikola Vaptsarov, Ivan Vazov, and Hristo Botev, hardly household names, are known to Esperantists through translations. The poetry of the Latvian Jānis Rainis, or of the Icelander Thorsteinn frá Hamri, or the prose of Friesland and Catalonia are accessible to Esperantists, although the non-Esperantist public hardly knows of their existence, or even of the languages in question. Thus Esperanto acts as a bridge between cultures. It is the Esperanto version of *Marta* that has been translated into Chinese and Japanese, and the Esperanto text of *Kon-Tiki* that has served as the source of several further translations. Retranslation is, of course, a limited phenomenon and likely to remain so; but in other fields, where style is less essential, it could be useful in various ways, for example providing translations from the major scientific languages into other languages, as has already been suggested by several language-conscious people in the third world. It would be a great advantage for all those who are not native speakers of one of the hegemonic Western languages to be able to read scientific works originally written in English, French, or Russian without the necessity of first learning those languages—a major stumbling block between such readers and the sources of scientific information.

The previous chapter has shown us how the flexibility of Esperanto makes it readily adaptable to the spirit of the original text. However, translation into Esperanto requires as much care and sensitivity as translation into any other language: the fact that Esperanto is easy to learn by no means implies that translation into it or out of it is particularly easy. It simply means (and this is a valuable advantage) that the translator can concentrate on the fundamentals of the art of translation, namely the adequate conveying of sense and form, without losing time and effort over the often arbitrary complications and idiomatic difficulties of ethnic languages. In practice, the specific advantage of Esperanto lies in the fact that translators generally work from their native language into Esperanto, thus reversing the usual procedure of going from a language foreign to them (even if they have perfect command over it) into their mother tongue. Thus the translation conveys a more direct understanding of the content and a finer appreciation of the beauties of the original. Only a Finn could give to the *Kalevala* that fidelity down to the last syllable that the translator Johan Leppäkoski provides. We are dealing here not with transposition from one language to another, but with an authentic mediation of the text tantamount to a secondary creation. Ultimately, however, the greatest single advantage of Esperanto as a language of translation is its ability to adapt itself so faithfully to Finnish as well as Hebrew, to Japanese as well as French.

ORIGINAL LITERATURE

The history of Esperanto literature is generally divided into three periods.[4] During the early years, to 1914, the new literature offered Esperantists a field in which to experiment and to try out their linguistic theories. Although the language was much enriched by numerous translations, Esperantists also sought to perfect their medium and demonstrate its equality with national languages by trying their hand at original poetry. Such work was largely the product of activists eager to convince the world of the value of Esperanto, rather than of artists seeking self-expression, though several writers showed considerable talent. The second period covers the years between the two world wars, a period of adolescent crisis for the new literature, in which Ancients did battle with Moderns and the figures of Kálmán Kalocsay and Gyula (Julio) Baghy presided over the scene. The period ended in a kind of didactic classicism. Since 1945 the blossoming of literary talent on five continents attests to the fact that Esperanto literature has entered a highly creative phase and is regarded as a normal and essential part of the Esperanto scene.

The First Period

Unlike the numerous translations produced by Zamenhof, and by Antoni Grabowski, Vasili Devyatnin, Abraham Kofman, and Kabe (Kazimierz Bein), the *Fundamenta krestomatio*, an anthology compiled by Zamenhof himself, had a purely normative goal. Zamenhof wrote in the preface,

> As a purely conventional means of intercommunication, the international language, like any national language, will not achieve its goal unless everyone uses it in the same way; and for everyone to use it in the same way, there must be certain

normative models that all accept as guides. That is why, in response to requests from numerous Esperantists, I have published the *Fundamenta krestomatio*, which can serve as a model of Esperanto style for all, and keep the language from the danger of degeneration into separate dialects. [OV 42]

The writers of this period were primarily translators, theoreticians, or propagandists. The Slavs showed a particular interest in stylistic freedom, and among them appeared some of the earliest genuine talents. In addition to Zamenhof's brother Felix (1868–1933), we should mention Antoni Grabowski (1857–1921), a Polish chemist and author of various scientific works, who could translate from thirty languages and who, with Zamenhof, apparently participated in the first conversation in the international language. His poems *"Tagiĝo"* (Daybreak), *"Reveno de l'filo"* (Return of the Son), and *"Sur unu kordo"* (On One String) are classic anthology texts, but his influence was more linguistic than literary, although his translations of *Pan Tadeusz* (Adam Mickiewicz) and *Mazepa* (Juliusz Słowacki) won him a reputation as father of poetic language in Esperanto.

Leo Belmont (1865–1941), a Polish journalist, published a collection of poems, *Sonoj Esperantaj* (1908), as well as numerous spirited essays. Vasili Devyatnin (1862–1938), a teacher of Latin and Russian literature, was the pioneer of Esperanto literature in Russia. His collected works in four volumes (1906–1911) contain original poems and stories, along with translations of Pushkin. Devyatnin also wrote an account of a journey on foot from Paris to Krakow in 1912. Alexander Dambrauskas (1860–1940), a Lithuanian Catholic priest, published, under the name Dombrowski, religious poems which maintain their simplicity despite the afflictions of persecution. Pál Lengyel (1868–1932), a Hungarian printer who emigrated to France, published his *Libro de l'humorajo* (Book of Humor) and, in his memoirs, recounted the more somber story of his own life. The Russian teacher Ivan Shiryaev (1877–1933) was the initiator of the *Enciklopedio de Esperanto* (1933), for which he compiled over two thousand articles. He also left short stories and translations. Stanislas Schulhof (1864–1919), a Czech dentist, was the first poet whose lyric talent truly coincided with the spirit of the international language. *Petaloj* (Petals) by Czeslaw Kozlowski, and *Unuaj agordoj* (First Tunings), by Stanislaw Braun and Stanislaw Karolczyk, consist of youthful pieces, melancholy in tone, which did not lead to more mature work.

The French influence, primarily intellectual and middle-class, was more apparent in organizational than in artistic matters. The mathematicians Charles Méray and Carlo Bourlet, General Hippolyte Sébert, Louis Chevreux (alias de Beaufront), and the philosopher Emile Boirac used their influence and extensive contacts for the benefit of Esperanto, and there were soon two Esperanto journals in France: *La Revuo*, published by Hachette under the editorship of Carlo Bourlet, and *Lingvo Internacia*, edited by Théophile Cart. These two journals were the first to emphasize the opposition between innovative, progressive, and inventive tendencies in language and movement (epitomized in the former) and orthodoxy and conservatism (revealed in the latter)—tendencies that were to remain an important part of Esperanto's history.

Of course, during this first period textbooks and dictionaries abounded, along with the first scientific essays in the language, among them those by the Swiss René de Saussure (brother of the linguist Ferdinand). Among literary works, we should also mention the two novels by Henri Vallienne (1854–1909), *Kastelo de Prelongo* (The Castle of Prelongo, 1907) and *Ĉu li?* (Is it him? 1908). They display a wonderful inventiveness and ability to create suspense, in a genre that has yet to be fully developed in Esperanto. Under the pseudonym Roksano, Jeanne Flourens (1871–1928) defended, with suffragist fervor, the view that writers should use only the words contained in the *Fundamento*, turning her theory into practice in the writing of humorous sketches. It was left to Reinhold Schmidt to set the first important landmark in the history of Esperanto theater in a five-act drama, *Gustaf Vasa* (1910). Finally, during this period Edmond Privat (1889–1962) began a long and versatile career devoted to Esperanto. He was Zamenhof's first biographer and also the first historian of the Esperanto movement. A poet of delicate sensitivity from his early years, he published *Tra l'silento* (Through the Silence) in 1912. As a dramatist, in *Ginevra*, he showed more lyricism than dramatic talent. Privat explored the expressive qualities of the language in a small volume entitled *Esprimo de sentoj en Esperanto* (The Expression of Feelings in Esperanto). He was also a talented orator who knew, like Boirac in France, how to use his position in the Swiss university system to disseminate Esperanto.

The Second Period

Esperanto ceased to be a novelty in the eyes of the public. After the formation of the League of Nations, which in effect concerned itself officially with the realization of the humanitarian goal of Esperantism, the movement's publicity insisted less on its idealistic aims and more on the practical possibilities of the language. As before, numerous translations continued to appear, but two new currents emerged in this second period.

First, a scientific approach to the language developed among linguistic theoreticians, who came to view it as an object of research. Esperantology, or Esperanto studies, was thus born, and practitioners included distinguished lexicographers such as Emile Grosjean-Maupin, Eugen Wüster, and Gaston Waringhien, and grammarians like Waringhien and Kálmán Kalocsay, who compiled, in Esperanto, the monumental two-volume *Plena gramatiko de Esperanto* (1935–1938), revised as *Plena analiza gramatiko de Esperanto* (Complete Analytical Grammar of Esperanto, 1980). Controversies erupted over questions of morphology and syntax, involving, in addition to those just mentioned, Teo Jung, Tomas Pumpr, and Théophile Cart. In 1931 Ernest Drezen published his *Historio de la mondolingvo* (History of the World Language), which remains the most sophisticated history of planned languages. A two-volume *Enciklopedio de Esperanto*, as we have already noted, appeared in Budapest in 1933, under the editorship of Lajos Kökény and with over fifty contributors. Petro Stojan compiled one of the fundamental reference works for interlinguistics, *Bibliografio de internacia lingvo* (1929, rep. 1973), and Johannes Dietterle compiled the *Originala verkaro* (Collected Original Works) of Zamenhof, published in the same year, the standard edition until the recent publication of the multivolume collection edited by Ludovikito (Kanzi Itô). These various works provided the first significant milestone on the way to the scholarly study of Esperanto.

The second major current was that of literature, which came to its maturity in this second period. Literary activity was no longer the exclusive domain of amateurs, but took on a professional tone among writers whose work extended over several decades and displayed qualities comparable with those of writers in ethnic languages. The Budapest School, centered on the journal *Literatura Mondo* (Literary World, founded 1922), included ten or more authors who played an important part in the original literature of Esperanto.

Julio Baghy (1891–1967), actor, director, and tireless enthusiast for the "internal idea," wrote as a compassionate, antiwar poet in *Preter la vivo* (Beyond Life, 1923), *Pilgrimo* (1962), and *La vagabondo kantas* (The Vagabond Sings, 1933), as a satiric, somewhat pessimistic short-story writer in *Dancu marionetoj* (Dance, Marionettes, 1927), *Verdaj donkiĥotoj* (Green Don Quixotes, 1933), *La teatra korbo* (The Costume Hamper, 1924), *Koloroj* (1926), and *Migranta plumo* (Wandering Pen, 1929), and as a talented novelist on war in *Viktimoj* (1925) and *Sur sanga tero* (On Blood-Soaked Earth, 1933) and on utopia in *Hura* (1930). His three-act lyrical drama *Sonĝe sub pomarbo* (Dreaming under an Apple Tree, 1956) looks to a technological future through the prism of youthful fantasy.

Kálmán Kalocsay (1891–1976), physician, university professor, and editor-in-chief of *Literatura mondo*, became well known for his numerous and accomplished translations and his essays on language (*Lingvo stilo formo*, 1931), as well as for his collaboration in the *Plena gramatiko* and *Parnasa gvidlibro* (Guidebook to Parnassus, 1932). In his poetry, like Grabowski before him, he introduced a number of neologisms, thereby reviving the dispute between the supporters of a minimum or maximum Esperanto. Kalocsay did much to advance the maximalist cause, and most of his neologisms now have a place in the dictionary. *Streĉita kordo* (Taut String, 1931), *Rimportretoj* (Portraits in Rhyme, 1931), and *Izolo* (Isolation; poems written between 1931 and 1939 but published only in 1977) are stylistic and topical experiments designed to prove the adaptability of Esperanto to all poetic circumstances. Among the new writers Kalocsay introduced through *Literatura mondo* were Ferenc Szilágyi, Lajos Tárkony, Hendrik Adamson, Hilda Dresen, Brian Price Heywood, Nikolao Hovorka, Nikolai Kurzens, Georges Maura (Gaston Waringhien), Amalia Núñez Dubús, L. N. M. Newell, and others, whose work continued into the third, postwar period.

In Britain, the journal *International Language* (1923–1931) provided a focal point for Esperanto writers. Newell (1902–1968), mentioned above, wrote a small body of carefully crafted poetry, collected in 1987, and a volume of ironic short stories, *Bakŝiŝ* (1938). His retranslation of *Hamlet*, sixty years after Zamenhof's, demonstrates the stability and development of Esperanto in its first half century. K. R. C. Sturmer (1903–1960) was a writer of short stories on various subjects and in various styles, and figures unintentionally among the founders of Esperanto sociology through his *Notlibro de praktika esperantisto* (Notebook of a Practical Esperantist, 1934). H. A. Luyken (1864–1940) revealed himself as a somewhat conventional moralist in four novels: *Paŭlo Debenham* (1912), *Mirinda amo* (Wonderful Love, 1913), *Stranga heredaĵo* (Strange Inheritance, 1922), and *Pro Iŝtar* (For Ishtar, 1924).

In the Soviet Union several talented writers emerged: the adventurous revolutionary E. Izgur, the Marxist essayist and poet Nikolai Nekrasov, and the poet Eugene Mihalski, whose brilliant linguistic discoveries are contained in several small volumes of poetry, including *Prologo* (1929) and *Fajro kuracas* (Fire Heals 1932). Vladimir Varankin, author of the study on interlinguistics *Teorio de Esperanto*, offers a realistic view of the crisis years in Berlin and Moscow in the well-known novel *Metropoliteno* (1933, English translation 1979). The only collection of poems by Nikolai Hohlov, *La tajdo* (The Tide, 1928), presents a poet of refined lyricism, worthy of a place in the Esperanto Parnassus next to the blind Vasiliy Eroshenko, Aleksandro Lilyer (Logvin), and Georgo Deshkin.

Other European countries also contributed. Germany offered the first crime novel in Esperanto, *Pro kio?* (For What? 1921) by Friedrich Wilhelm Ellersiek, who wrote under the name of Argus. The Netherlands produced a series of novels by Hindrik Bulthuis, *Idoj de Orfeo* (Offspring of Orpheus, 1923), *La vila mano* (The Hairy Hand, 1928), and *Inferio* (Country of Hell, 1938). Stellan Engholm (1899–1960) of Sweden published a trilogy of novels—*Al Torento* (To Torento), *Infanoj en Torento* (Children in Torento), and *Vivo vokas* (Life Calls)—and a fourth novel, *Homoj sur la tero* (Humans on the Earth, 1932), in which he chronicles the life of a rural family through three generations. In Poland, Jean Forge (Jan Fethke) began his career as humorist with three sensitive and observant novels, *Abismoj* (1923), *Saltego trans jarmiloj* (Leap across Millennia, 1924), and *Mister Tot aĉetas mil okulojn* (Mister Tot Buys a Thousand Eyes, 1931). Catalonia has its self-styled troubadours Jaume Grau Casas and Artur Domenech y Mas, and France is represented by a first-rate humorist in the cabaret tradition, Raymond Schwartz, a poet in *Verdkata testamento* (The Will of the Green Cat, 1926) and *La stranga butiko* (The Odd Shop, 1931), and a novelist in the brief *Anni kaj Montmartre* (1930) and in *Kiel akvo de l'rivero* (Like Water from the River, 1963), one of the few masterpieces in this genre in Esperanto. Schwartz also wrote the entertaining and amusing volumes *Prozo ridetanta* (Smiling Prose, 1928), *La ĝoja podio* (The Merry Stage, 1949), *Vole... novele* (Stories Willy Nilly, 1971) and *... Kun siaspeca spico* (With Its Own Kind of Spiciness, 1971). (See Bernard 1987.) Serious in tone and penetrating in subject matter, Norbert Bartelmes (1897–1987) is the most important literary offshoot of the circle around Lanti (Eugéne Adam), founder of the "non-nationalist" movement Sennacieca Asocio Tutmonda (SAT). He produced a translation of *Faust*, numerous articles, short stories ("*Ne plu ludo,*" No Longer a Game, 1973), and two novels, *Juneca ardo* (Youthful Ardor, 1936) and *Vartejoj* (Nurseries, 1938), concerned with education, freedom, and class consciousness. Along with Varankin and the Englishman K. R. C. Sturmer (Kenelm Robinson), famous for the brief novel *Por recenzo!* (For Review, 1930), the collection of stories *Se grenereto* (If the Tiniest Grain, 1932) and the brief play *Homaranisma laboro* (1931), Bartelmes can be regarded as representative of the freethinking tradition that flourished in Europe in the period before the Second World War.

The Third Period

Literary creation, temporarily interrupted by the war, soon revived, thanks to the major writers of the Budapest School, which in turn inspired a new, so-called Scottish school. This productive period was marked by a proliferation of journals and intense publishing activity that, in addition to an increasing number of translations, to which the countries of East Asia also now contributed, saw the appearance of new writers in a wider range of countries than before. Today, the study of Esperanto literature has become a major critical undertaking, and it is no longer sufficient simply to classify increasing numbers of authors by genre and talent. There is in fact a risk that the more productive writers will overshadow other talents who, although minor in terms of quantity, display in their poems and stories (scattered in magazines and literary competitions), qualities equal to those of the better-known authors. In the following section we shall be unable to explore all, or even all the most valuable, of the current writers in Esperanto, but will confine ourselves to providing a brief sketch of current trends.

As before, Hungarian writers stand out. Ferenc Szilágyi, to whom we alluded above, emigrated to Sweden, where he became editor of the distinguished journal *Norda Prismo* (Northern Prism) from 1955 to 1967 and published three short story collections, *La granda aventuro* (1945), *Inter sudo kaj nordo* (1950), and *Koko krias jam* (The Cock Is Already Crowing, 1955), along with the crime novel *Mistero minora* (Mystery in Minor Key, 1958). Sándor Szathmári (1897–1974), author of the science fiction novel *Vojaĝo al Kazohinio* (1958, English translation *Kazohinia*, 1975), wrote this Swiftian satire on a perfectly rational society in the years before the war, but produced short stories somewhat similar in tone in the postwar period, published in *Maŝinmondo* (Machine World, 1964) and *Kain kaj Abel* (1977) and collected as *Perfekta civitano* (Perfect Citizen, 1988). Imre Baranyai (1902–1961), who wrote under the name Emba, published the novel *Maria kaj la grupo* in 1936 but is best remembered as a poet (*Ekzilo kaj azilo*, Exile and Refuge, 1962).

Britain's reputation lies particularly with the Scottish school: J. S. Dinwoodie, Reto Rossetti, John Islay Francis, and William Auld published their joint volume of poetry, *Kvaropo*, in 1952, acknowledging their kinship with Kalocsay and Grabowski. Of the four, Auld is the most prolific and experimental; his *La infana raso* (The Infant Race, 1958) stands in sharp contrast to his somber lyricism in *Unufingraj melodioj* (One-Finger Melodies, 1960). A collected edition of his poems has appeared recently (1987). Rossetti, in addition to a small volume of witty, often parodic, poems, *Pinta krajono* (Sharp Pencil, 1959), wrote the short stories in *El la maniko* (Out of My Sleeve, 1955) in a scintillating linguistic style. Francis, less concerned with language, has achieved classic status through his short stories in *Vitralo* (Stained-Glass Window, 1960), in which complex symbolism and a fine sense of the dramatic put him in the first rank of Esperanto short-story writers. His extensive novels *La granda kaldrono* (The Great Cauldron, 1978) and *Misio sen alveno* (Mission without

Return, 1982) are important additions to the growing list of accomplished Esperanto novels. Marjorie Boulton has also alternated poetry (*Kontralte*, In Contralto Voice, 1955; *Eroj, Pieces*, 1959; *Cent ĝojkantoj*, A Hundred Carols, 1957) and prose: sketches, a biography of Zamenhof (English edition 1960, Esperanto edition 1962), and short stories in *Okuloj* (Eyes, 1967), and *Dekdu piedetoj* (Twelve Little Feet, 1964)—all displaying the successful linkage of style and feeling. To this list of English-speaking Esperanto writers we should add the New Zealander Brendon Clark (1904–1956), whose particular poetic theories (*Kien la poezio?* Whither Poetry? 1957) lie at the opposite extreme from the Scottish school in their resistance to neologisms and poetic language, and Bertram Potts, also from New Zealand, writer of short stories alternating humor and suspense in *Nokto da timo* (Night of Fear, 1971), *La nova butikisto de Nukugaia* (The New Shopkeeper of Nukugaia, 1978), and *Kaverno apud la maro* (Cave beside the Sea, 1985).

Controversies (both within and outside the movement), the expanding Esperanto periodical press and radio broadcasts, international congresses, public relations campaigns—all have brought with them their own literature in the form of essays, articles, and speeches. A special place belongs to Gaston Waringhien, a major figure also in our second period (see above), whose essays *Eseoj I: Beletro* (Essays I: Belles Lettres, 1956), *Lingvo kaj vivo* (Life and Language, 1969), *Ni kaj ĝi* (We and It, 1972), *1887 kaj la sekvo* (1887 and What Followed, 1980) and *Kaj la ceter'—nur literaturo* (And the Rest—Just Literature, 1983) are models of style, adding to Waringhien's distinction as lexicographer, grammarian, and poet (this last under the pseudonym Georges Maura). A good example of the genre of advocacy and polemics in Esperanto is contained in the speeches of Ivo Lapenna and the essays of Werner Bormann. Lapenna's *Retoriko* (1950) deals with the art of oratory. In the field of scholarship Esperanto has shown its suitability as an academic language in the work of Paul Neergaard, Alberto Fernandez, Sin'itiro Kawamura, Detlev Blanke, Tibor Sekelj, Atan Atanasov, John C. Wells, István Szerdahelyi, and dozens of other scholars.

Group meetings, congresses, and the teaching of the language have given birth to various light or didactic subgenres, some achieving artistic distinction. The writing of sketches has not developed into a true theatrical tradition in Esperanto and cannot compete with translated works, but, in its limited context, it is well adapted to the life and the theatrical possibilities of the movement. Professional theater companies, mostly young people, present them at the still infrequent festivals of Esperanto theater. Among those who have written sketches and one-act plays are Marjorie Boulton, Julio Baghy, J. D. Applebaum, Giorgio Silfer, Zora Heide, E. V. Tvarožek, Emilija Lapenna, Karl Minor, Vittorio Dall'Acqua, J. and K. Filip, Stefan MacGill, the cabaret writers Bukar and Lorjak, and others. To these examples of writers of light entertainment, we should add Henri Baupierre, whose parodies, *Specimene*, were published in 1963; Louis Beaucaire, whose amusing stories of the imaginary village of Bervalo are widely read; and a growing and promising school of writers and performers of songs and ballads.

The writers of short stories in Esperanto are of high quality, and merit comparison with similar writers in ethnic languages. Jean Forge, whose career began in the second period, added two further collections of stories in the third: *La verda raketo* (The Green Racquet, 1961) and *Mia verda breviero* (My Green Breviary, 1974). The former is already regarded as a classic, and the latter collection draws on the same inspiration, humorous and satiric observation of the Esperanto movement. The Norwegian Johan Hammond Rosbach (*Bagatelaro*, Trifles, 1951; *Homoj kaj riveroj*, People and Rivers, 1957; *La mirinda eliksiro*, The Amazing Elixir, 1967; *Disko*, 1970) is an inventive writer with a sense of drama and a careful balance of reason and emotion. The Frenchman Jean Ribillard writes in exotic terms of the Arab world in *Vagado sub palmoj* (Wandering under Palms, 1956) and *Vivo kaj opinioj de majstro M'saud* (Life and Opinions of Master M'saud, 1963). Other countries in which new writers of short stories have emerged include Denmark (G. Riisberg, *Suno kaj pluvo*, Sun and Rain, 1972), Bulgaria (Nevena Nedelcheva, *Patrina koro*, A Mother's Heart; *Dum nokta deĵoro*, On Night Duty, 1987), Italy (Lina Gabrielli, *La kombilo*, The Comb, 1962; *Karnavalo*, 1973; *La ĝardeno de la urbestro*, The Mayor's Garden, 1978), Greece (Despina Patrinu, *Homa animo*, Human Soul, 1976), and Yugoslavia (Vesna Skaljer Race, *El la vivo*, From Life, 1977; Spomenka Štimec, *Vojaĝo al disiĝo*, Journey to Separation, 1990). A whole range of talent has emerged in recent years in Japan, beginning with Miyamoto Masao's *Pri arto kaj morto* (On Art and Life, 1967) and including the work of Yagi Nihei (*Mozaiko Tokio*, 1975),

Konisi Gaku (*Vage tra la dimensioj*, Wandering through the Dimensions, 1976) and Ueyama Masao (*Pardonon*, 1970; *Mi amas . . .*, I Love, 1977).[5]

The years following the war, indeed the period up to about 1975, showed only modest progress in the development of the Esperanto novel. H. L. Eggerup's *D-ro Dorner* appeared in 1945 and Stellan Engholm's *Vivo vokas* (Life Is Calling) in 1946, but they had few successors. Cezaro Rossetti's amusing novel *Kredu min, sinjorino* (Believe Me, Madam), the misadventures of a traveling salesman, appeared in 1950, and Margrid Thoraeus-Ekström's brief novel *Brilo de fantomo* (Brilliance of a Ghost) was published in 1967. While these novels were accompanied by the impressive contributions of Francis and Schwartz, and while they were not wholly alone, they hardly constituted a flowering of the novel. W. Verloren van Themaat's *La akvariinfanoj* (The Aquarium Children) appeared in 1976, the same year as the Japanese Kazuta Oka's *Matenruĝo* (Morning Red), a semiauto-biographical story of youth and the left, and Miyamoto Masao's impressive *Naskitaj sur la ruino* (Born on the Ruin), set in Okinawa.

The announcement in 1975 of the Raymond Schwartz Prize for the best new novel in Esperanto changed the picture completely. Intended as a stimulus to would-be novelists, it had precisely the desired effect. The prize was won by Éva Tófalvi and Oldrich Knichal for *Kiuj semas plorante . . .* (Those Who Sow with Tears . . . , 1980), a novel of World War II with an Esperantist theme. Karolo Piĉ of Czechoslovakia, a runner-up in the competition, published his dense experimental novel *La litomiŝla tombejo* (Litomišl Cemetery) in 1981, following it with two other complex works, *La mortsonorilo de Chamblay* (The Funeral Bell of Chamblay, 1983) and *Klaĉejo* (Place of Gossip, 1987). Piĉ was not alone in tackling difficult subjects. Spomenka Štimec's *Ombro sur interna pejzaĝo* (Shadow on an Inner Landscape, 1984) is a haunting semiautobiographical novel about the fragility of love, and Blazio Vaha's *Adolesko* (Adolescence, 1987) explores the past life of its Catholic author.

Kiuj semas plorante . . ., despite its somber subject, was popular in style. In this regard it resembled Douglas P. Boatman's *Kara diablino* (Dear Devil, 1979) a mystery story, and the extraordinarily popular humorous works of Lorjak, whose half dozen novels began in 1975 with *Neologisme*. Johán Valano, of Switzerland, produced the first of his five widely read crime novels

in 1976. With works such as these, Esperantists discovered
the pleasures of light reading in Esperanto, itself a sign of the
language's growing maturity, and after 1980 numerous titles
appeared. The Hungarian István Nemere, in a remarkable display
of creative talent, has published some ten novels in the past eight
years, beginning with *La fermita urbo* (The Closed City, 1982).
Others who have joined Nemere include Deck Dorval of the
Netherlands, with three novels to his credit, Corrado Tavanti of
Italy, with two, and Knichal, whose second novel appeared in ·
1987. Other recent novels include the work of, among others,
Julian Modest (Bulgaria), Mies Bouhuys (Netherlands), and
Manjo Austin (Britain). In fact, more novels have been published
in Esperanto in the past fifteen years or so than appeared in the
previous ninety.

During this same period poetry has seen a more gradual
evolution—largely away from schools of poets and toward the
emergence of individual talent. If British poets like Auld and
Boulton looked back to Kalocsay, Baghy, and Mihalski, they now
provide models for a younger generation. British poets emerging
over the past twenty years include Albert Goodheir (*Merlo sur
menhiro*, Blackbird on a Menhir, 1974; *Enlumiĝo*, Into the Light,
1987), Victor Sadler, whose startlingly original *Memkritiko* (Self-
Criticism) appeared in 1967 but has led to no further publication,
and Daphne Lister (*Ĝis nun*, Until Now, 1976). The German poet
and designer Richard Schulz stands in splendid isolation as
a master of short verse (pantoum, sonnet, limerick, Persian
quatrain). Perhaps the most outstanding younger talent to follow
in the footsteps of Auld and Kalocsay is the Italian Mauro Nervi
(*La turoj de la ĉefurbo*, The Towers of the Capital, 1978), who like
Kalocsay is a medical doctor. Among Nervi's inspirations is also
the Icelander Baldur Ragnarsson, a contemporary of Auld and
Boulton and a formidable poet and critic. Other Italian poets of
the period include Clelia Conterno Guglielminetti (*Eta vivo*, Little
Life, 1959), Lina Gabrielli (*Ni devas vivi*, We Must Live, 1975;
Vivendo, Need to Live, 1979), Nicolino Rossi (*Sur la vivopado*, On
the Path of Life, 1980), and Giorgio Silfer (*De tempo al tempo*,
From Time to Time, 1977). Aldo de'Giorgi's *Pretertempe* (Beyond
Time) appeared in 1982.

But every country of western Europe has its Esperanto
poets, some of limited range, some with whole lists of original
and translated work to their credit. As for eastern and central

Europe, recent events have opened up new opportunities for publication, especially in Russia, where something of a revival of creative writing and literary criticism is underway. Hilda Dresen, of Estonia, who died in 1981, began her career, along with several other poets in the Baltic States, in the period between the wars. She continued publishing throughout the Soviet period, but she was almost alone in doing so. Poland has been more hospitable to Esperanto poetry over the years, and in Czechoslovakia a whole range of poets has emerged, among them Tomáš Pumpr, Eli Urbanová, Štefo Urban, Karolo Pič, and Jiři Kořínek. Yugoslav poetry has been collected in two anthologies of original Esperanto work, *Reeĥoj* (Re-echoes, 1961), containing the work of nineteen poets, and a new collection from Croatia (1991) with twenty-two poets represented. In 1987 a large anthology of original Esperanto poetry from Bulgaria brought together selections from over sixty poets. Numerous individual volumes have also appeared.

Europe, however, no longer occupies center stage, and new developments are occurring constantly in other parts of the world. This situation represents a significant realignment in the evolution of Esperanto poetry. Saint-Jules Zee (Xu Shengyue) of China and Dan Tirinaro of Korea long ago served as harbingers of this rising talent in Asia. Zee's poems appeared in Western literary journals between the wars and he was one of nine poets represented in a collection published by Literatura Mondo in Budapest in 1938. Burgeoning talents in Japan during this period were engulfed by the rising tide of nationalism, but in the post-war period they reemerged, led by Ossaka Kenji (*El orienta florbedo*, From an Eastern Garden, 1956), and especially Miyamoto Masao (*Invit' al japanesko*, Invitation to Japanesery, 1971). The Japanese group known as the Haiku Club—Ueyama Masao, Kuroda Masayuki, Yamada Tempu, Tanaka Sadami, and others, including Miyamoto—breathed new life into a somewhat tired poetic form in a series of six annual volumes (1967–1973) of delicate technique and sensibility. Ueyama and Kuroda have both subsequently published volumes of their own.

The South African Edwin de Kock has published a total of six collections of his poetry, beginning in 1961 with *Ombroj de la kvara dimensio* (Shadows of the Fourth Dimension). While interested in experiment, de Kock is above all a poet of carefully crafted lyrics. But he is a lonely voice on the African continent. Nor have southern and western Asia produced their poets, apart from an occasional Israeli voice. Latin America, however, is another matter, and Brazil, particularly, occupies an important place in modern Esperanto poetry. Perhaps the most impressive of the Brazilian poets is Geraldo Mattos, whose *Miniaturoj* (1959) was heavily influenced by Japanese models. Indeed, fixed form has remained the particular talent of Mattos, whose sonnets, *Arĉoj*, appeared in 1967 and have been followed by two further sonnet cycles, *La libro de adoro* (The Book of Adoration) and *La libro de Nejma* (Nejma's Book), both in 1985. Taking seriously Zamenhof's appeal to writers, back at the beginning of Esperanto, that they tackle difficult tasks, Mattos also produced the verse drama *Ivan VI* (1953). Sylla Chaves, whose *Animo prisma* (Prismatic Soul), appeared in 1959, Diderto Freto (*Monosilaboj*, 1967, 1972, 1985, 1990), and Roberto Passos Nogueira (*Vojo kaj vorto*, Way and Word, 1972) are, along with Mattos, only the most important of a flourishing group of writers now publishing in Brazil.

We cannot conclude even this extremely rapid overview without highlighting the role of literary magazines and publishers. Among the former we should cite the historically important *Literatura mondo*, published in Hungary from the 1920s into the 1940s, *Norda prismo*, published in Scandinavia, and *Nica literatura revuo*, published in France. All three magazines have now passed into history, along with numerous others in Japan, Yugoslavia, and elsewhere, but new periodicals have arrived to take their place, notably *Literatura foiro*, now published in Italy, and *Fonto*, in Brazil. Such general interest magazines as *Hungara vivo*, after thirty years a recent victim of rising costs in Hungary, and *La gazeto* (France) have also played a part, while new literary magazines in the former Soviet Union, modestly produced, have revived interest and opportunity there.

As for publishers, Literatura Mondo, in Budapest, was the principal literary outlet in the 1920s and 1930s, a role assumed after the war by Juan Régulo Pérez, whose small publishing house in the Canary Islands, Stafeto, published many of the writers we have mentioned above.[6] Fonto (Brazil) and Edistudio (Italy) have now assumed a somewhat similar role.

A literature is only as accessible as its publishers, and the particular geographical distribution of talent described above may be as much a function of the availability of outlets and of a public able to buy books as it is of native ability or cultural context. Today, as many as a hundred publishers East and West sustain the culture of the Esperanto movement with books and with monthly or quarterly magazines and journals. Even in the most prosaic or modest among them, there is often a literary section, or a story or a poem. In contrast to the national-language press, which generally separates literature from information and deals with the former in specialized periodicals, the Esperantist desire for an aesthetic artistic language is expressed in varying degrees throughout the periodical press, attesting to the linguistic and cultural sophistication of its readers.

SOME CONCLUSIONS ON THE LITERARY PHENOMENON IN ESPERANTO

In the history of Esperanto literature we can observe three more or less interconnected stages. During the first period, writers were concerned chiefly with advocacy and wished to prove that Esperanto was a language equal in quality to the ethnic languages, capable of performing the same functions. This advocacy phase is accordingly closely linked with the second, experimental phase, characterized by linguistic research, refinement, experimentation. Finally, the fully developed language was ready for the third phase, in which it is employed to express original content, either individual or collective. The three phases overlap, but it is fair to say that, today, writers who choose Esperanto make their choice on the basis of artistic criteria. It would be foolish to deny the importance of this choice and its literary implications. It means that Esperanto does not function only at the level of instrumental communication—and what would be the good of an international language that did only that, as if it were not possible to learn enough English or Russian or Chinese to ask the price of a room and what time breakfast is served?—nor does it only reach the level of scientific or commercial transactions, though, to be sure, its precision facilitates them. A century of experience has given us clear proof that a planned language can express everything worthy of expression, provided that it creates and nurtures its own spirit. With respect to art and beauty, there is nothing artificial about the structure of the language. Faced with the success of Esperanto writers and the aesthetic level of their works, it would be absurd to declare that Esperanto literature is artificial. "Is Esperanto destined to produce works of art, to give tongue to literary masterpieces?" the famous French writer Georges Duhamel wondered aloud some years ago in an interview with Pierre Delaire. And he answered his own question: "I believe that Esperanto could one day bring forth extraordinary works destined for a wide and various audience."[7]

Of course, the quality of this literature varies. The novel is still not fully developed as a genre. Writers for the theater are lacking, though theater companies do now exist. But there are good short story writers, poets, and songwriters. An Esperanto Shakespeare or Dante has yet to arise, but no linguistic or artistic obstacle prevents this from happening. Very few nations, furthermore, can claim such an illustrious roster of authors, and many of the languages spoken today and claiming a written literature cannot demonstrate such valuable achievements as Esperanto literature.

There exist documentary and advertising films in Esperanto. The first fictional films were produced by J. L. Mahé (*Angoroj*, 1966) and by Paramount Pictures (*Incubus*, 1966).[8]

Esperanto writers have played a critical role in determining the future of the language. They have enriched and perfected the lexicon and the basic grammar. They have explored its possibilities and exploited its potential. They have developed a language capable of fulfilling all the functions of the most developed national languages and superior to them in its almost limitless adaptability. As Zamenhof foresaw, neologisms are pushing out archaisms, but that shows that Esperanto is evolving like all living creatures (and all living languages) according to its own dynamics. This vitalization of a project that could have remained as lifeless as the many other language projects constitutes a remarkable linguistic event that cannot be ignored.

In the field of literature, it is important because it proves that a planned language is not only capable of cultural and artistic communication but also capable of creating art and culture. With respect to literature, Esperanto has a unique characteristic: although it is not the native language of the writer, the writer does not feel it to be foreign. Because of the absence of arbitrary obstacles (illogical construction, idiomatic expressions, incomprehensible rules) a writer acquires perfect mastery over the language, and this guarantees total self-expression in fully expressive language. But the Esperanto writer is not simply a perfectly bilingual author or an author in a second language; nor is this writer entirely comparable with, let us say, an English poet writing in Japanese. Crossing from his or her own language into Esperanto, the writer does not leave one native system in order to enter another with equally known yet equally tyrannical laws. Although Esperanto has its rules, they are few, and they do not force the artist into a straitjacket; furthermore, they are supple enough to reproduce as many linguistic structures as possible—as we have already shown. This means that the Esperanto writer must indeed observe, for example, the accusative, but that the rules governing the accusative allow the expression of the most varied linguistic structures so easily and adequately that for a writer Esperanto does not seem strange or foreign, but rather a kind of extension or completion of that writer's native language. This specific quality has brought many talented people to the international language and will probably attract more and more creative artists to the ranks of the Esperantists.[9]

Chapter 6

The Esperanto Movement

The results described in the previous chapter would not have been achieved without a large enough public and without organizations capable of steadily expanding the Esperanto movement. It is almost impossible to calculate the size of that movement. To understand how difficult a task it is, we should compare it not with a census of duly registered citizens, but with an effort to arrive at an approximate figure for a collection of totally unregistered individuals. Assessing the number of Esperantists in the world is like calculating the number of music lovers or sports enthusiasts. Two rough and ready methods allow us to arrive at some kind of estimate. The more direct consists in adding up the membership of all Esperanto organizations (at least 120,000 in 1987), but obviously not all Esperantists join an Esperanto association, and many enthusiasts become members in several.[1] Furthermore, membership is not necessarily synonymous with being an Esperantist: there exist members simply sympathetic to

113

the cause ("Esperantists without Esperanto" with small or non-existent knowledge of the language), but we also come upon nonmembers with a high level of linguistic competence. We must therefore supplement the direct method with another method, taking into consideration the social, economic, and political phenomena in which Esperantists participate. For example, in 1966 a proposal in support of Esperanto, presented to the United Nations by the Universal Esperanto Association, gathered 920,954 individual signatures and was also signed by 3,843 organizations on behalf of some 71 million members. If we suppose that one-tenth of these 72 million interested parties might be Esperanto users, the number of such users would exceed 7 million. If we accept a lower figure, say one-twentieth or one-fortieth, the number is still 3.5 million or almost 2 million, respectively. We might ask ourselves whether the organizations in question would feel able to sign a petition on behalf of their members, or would even be interested in doing so, if only a tiny proportion (2.5 percent if we take the lowest of the above figures) were Esperantists or Esperanto supporters.

This estimate, although hypothetical, is more realistic than the more direct method. But certain difficult questions remain. What kinds of Esperantists should be included in the estimate? Should we include only those who speak the language perfectly, and not the "eternal beginners"? Is an Esperantist only a person who regularly speaks, writes, reads, composes, thinks in Esperanto, or also a person who uses the language only occasionally but equally well? The criteria are imprecise and altogether elastic. Depending on what means of measurement we use, the estimate can vary between a strict but minimum figure of some 300,000 to a maximum but overgenerous number of some 15 million.

Although the question of numbers is important for a minority language, it should not overshadow achievements that cannot be measured numerically. To judge the influence and progress of the Esperanto movement, it is not enough to look at how many members it has, but what they actually do. The works of Mao in Esperanto were published in hundreds of thousands of copies at a time when the Chinese Esperanto League had only five hundred members. Certain Esperanto textbooks and dictionaries for Polish speakers sell out quickly, although the average print run is 20,000, while the Polish Esperanto Association, until recently one of the strongest, has a membership of only a little over six thousand members. The best way to calculate the strength of the entire Esperanto movement is to study its dynamics, as these are revealed in its internal structure and its various activities.

ORGANIZATION

Esperantists have, from the beginning, formed local associations (the oldest being that of Nuremberg, founded in 1888) for advocacy purposes as well as to practice the language; these, in turn, have established national associations. In 1991 there were national Esperanto associations in sixty-six countries. While these national associations play an important role in informing and teaching the public, the international associations work with world organizations like the United Nations and UNESCO. However, relatively few of the international associations are strong enough to function effectively at that level. Most of them are specialized organizations with professional, scientific, ideological, or leisure-time interests. The largest of the international associations is the Universal Esperanto Association (UEA), whose head office is in Rotterdam and which has some 40,000 members (1987). It declares itself neutral on political and religious matters. It has official representatives in seventy-two countries through its network of so-called delegates, or local representatives (over three thousand in all) and its forty-seven affiliated national associations. It has a youth section, the World Esperanto Youth Organization (*Tutmonda Esperantista Junulara Organizo*, TEJO), with an important host system for travelers.[2] Because virtually all the larger national associations and six of the specialized associations have affiliated with UEA, and thirty-two additional specialized associations have contracts of cooperation with it, the Universal Esperanto Association is the most prestigious standard-bearer of Esperanto worldwide. It publishes two attractive journals, *Esperanto* and *Kontakto*, assorted documents, and an impressive yearbook, which is itself an essential document for the most active Esperantists. Its annual World Congress provides non-Esperantists with an opportunity to observe firsthand the suitability of Esperanto as a means of international communication.

Another international association, *Sennacieca Asocio*

Tutmonda (Worldwide Non-national Association, SAT), occupies a special place in the movement. Founded in 1921 by the Frenchman Lanti with the aim of using Esperanto by and for the working class, SAT is the most original movement to have arisen from Zamenhof's *homaranismo*, since it deals directly with the political implications and consequences of the idea of a common language for the largest part of humanity—working people. Although its membership numbers only a little over three thousand, it is one of the more important driving forces in the movement because of the high level of language proficiency of its members and its extensive publishing activity.

In the specialized associations, Esperanto is adapted to specific technical tasks and is disseminated within specific professional or ideological circles. Four of these associations were created in the earliest years of Esperantism, three came into being between 1918 and 1939, and the others were founded after 1945. The following are the most important:

(Information is given in the following order: Area of specialization, name in Esperanto, country of secretariat. *Int.* = *Internacia*; *E* = *Esperanto*.)
Agriculture. *Int. ligo de agrikulturaj specialistoj-esperantistoj*. Bulgaria.
Arts. *Universala artista ligo de esperantistoj*. Finland.
Atheism. *Ateista tutmonda E-organizo*. USA.
Automobile Owners. *Int. E-klubo aŭtomobilista*. Hungary.
Baha'i. *Bahaa E-ligo*. Luxemburg.
Biblical and Oriental Studies. *Int. asocio de bibliistoj kaj orientalistoj*. Italy.
Biology. *Asocio por la enkonduko de nova biologia nomenklaturo*. Belgium.
Blind. *Ligo int. de blindaj esperantistoj*. Hungary.
Catholicism. *Int. katolika unuiĝo esperantista*. Italy.
Chess. *Esperanta ŝak-ligo int.* Germany.
Communism. *Kolektivo esperantista komunista*. Italy.
Comparative Religion. *Asocio de studado int. pri spiritaj kaj teologiaj instruoj*. France.
Computer Science. *Komputila rondo*. Germany.
Cooperativism. *Int. kooperativa E-organizo*. Hungary.
Cybernetics and Information Science. *Tutmonda asocio pri kibernetiko, informadiko, kaj sistemiko*. Czechoslovakia.
Cycling. *Biciklista esperantista movado int.* Netherlands.
Ecology. *Asocio de verduloj esperantistaj*. Belgium.
Economics. *Int. komerca kaj ekonomia fakgrupo*. Belgium.
Ecumenism. *Tutmonda ekumena ligo*. Greece.

Environment. *Tutmonda unio por vivprotektado, E-sekcio.* Austria.
Ethnic Freedoms. *Int. komitato por etnaj liberecoj.* Germany.
European Affairs. *Eŭropa klubo.* Germany
Gays. *Ligo de samseksamaj geesperantistoj.* U.K.
Go (Japanese game). *Esperantista go-ligo int.* Japan.
Handicapped. *Int. asocio de handikapitaj esperantistoj.* Yugoslavia.
Hexagonal Chess. *Int. esperantista heksa-ŝaka klubo.* Belarus.
Journalism. *Tutmonda esperantista ĵurnalista asocio.* Italy.
Law. *Int. E-asocio de juristoj.* Austria.
Librarians. *Tutmonda Esperanta bibliotekista asocio.* Netherlands.
Mathematics. *Int. asocio de esperantistaj matematikistoj.* France.
Medicine. *Universala medicina E-asocio.* Japan.
Mensa. *Espermenso.* Netherlands.
Miners. *Int. minista E-societo.* Poland.
Mormons. *Por-Esperanta mormonaro.* Belgium.
Music. *Muzika E-ligo.* Bulgaria.
Naturism. *Int. naturista organizo esperantista.* Belgium.
Oomoto (Japanese religion). *E-propaganda asocio de Oomoto.* Japan.
Peace. *Mondpaca esperantista movado.* France.
Philately. *E-ligo filatelista.* Sweden.
Philology. *Int. unuiĝo de la esperantistoj-filologoj.* Bulgaria.
Philosophy. *Filozofia asocio tutmonda.* Brazil.
Photography and Film. *Int. ligo de esperantistaj foto-kino-magnetofon-amatoroj.* Bulgaria.
Post and Telecommunication. *Int. poŝtista kaj telekomunikista E-asocio.* Bulgaria.
Protestants. *Kristana esperantista ligo int.* Netherlands.
Quakers. *Kvakera esperantista societo.* U.K.
Radio Amateurs. *Int. ligo de esperantistaj radio-amatoroj.* Hungary.
Radio Listeners. *E-DX-Club.* Germany.
Railways. *Int. fervojista E-federacio.* Italy.
Rock Music. *E-rok-asocio.* France.
Rotary. *Rotaria asocio de esperantistoj.* U.K.
Science. *Int. scienca asocio esperantista.* Norway.
Scouts. *Skolta E-ligo.* U.K.
Speleology. *Speleologia fakgrupo.* Czechoslovakia.
Spiritualism. *Spirita eldona societo F. V. Lorenz.* Brazil.
Stenography. *Tutmonda parolspuro-asocio.* Germany.
Teachers. *Int. ligo de esperantistaj instruistoj.* Sweden.
Terminology. *Terminologia Esperanto-centro.* Czechoslovakia.
Tourism. *Int. asocio monda turismo.* Poland.
Translation. *Int. tradukreto pere de E.* France.
UNESCO Affairs. *Monda kunagado por eduko, scienco, kaj kulturo.* Netherlands.

Vegetarianism. *Tutmonda esperantista vegetarana asocio*. Italy.
Veteran Esperantists. *Veterana esperantista klubo*. Denmark.
Writers. *Esperanta verkista asocio*. Netherlands.
Yoga. *Jogo en E*. Denmark.

Some of these specialized associations have no more than a hundred members, and even the largest have no more than 1500. However, their number is increasing steadily (since 1950, approximately eleven associations have been added to the existing number every ten years) and a few are engaged in outstanding publishing activities despite their modest financial resources. The scientific association, for example, has published a "Who's Who in Science and Technology" and the Association of Biblical and Oriental Studies is at work on an ecumenical translation of the Bible.

We must emphasize once again that the bare numbers are merely indicative and relative, though even in these terms they show considerable progress in the organizational life of the Esperanto movement. The neutral association UEA can also claim a steadily growing membership, from 30,185 in 1960, to 32,673 in 1975, to 39,005 in 1984, and 43,642 in 1987. There has been a parallel increase in attendance figures at world congresses. Although numbers vary from year to year depending on geographical and economic factors, we note that from 1953 on, the maximums have risen steadily: 3,256 in Warsaw in 1959; 3,472 in Sofia in 1963; 3,975 in Budapest in 1966; 4,414 in Varna in 1978; 4,887 in Budapest in 1983; and 5,946 in Warsaw in 1987. The minimum size has stayed at about 1,200 participants, and the average since 1952 is about 2,200. During this period the largest congresses took place in Poland, Bulgaria, and Hungary because these countries could be reached from both Eastern and Western Europe (travel to Western countries was often difficult for Easterners). We might also note that the attractiveness of these various congresses on the one hand and the strength of the local Esperantist base on the other is equally strong in various parts of the world, with the congresses in Havana (1990), Brasilia (1981), Madrid (1968), and Tokyo (1965) each attracting about 1,700 people.

Although these figures show steady progress in the organized life of the movement, they represent only one aspect of Esperantism. Esperantism as a whole must be judged in terms of the number and volume of its activities that reflect its specific goals: to solve the language problem in international communication, to facilitate all spiritual and material relations among people, and to develop among them understanding and esteem for other peoples. Such a judgment cannot be arrived at through precise numbers, and we must be content with general social indicators.

ACTIVITIES

Among the high-level activities launched out of the offices of UEA in Rotterdam and New York, the national and regional activities coordinated by the national associations, and the informal meetings of local clubs, where many Esperantists regularly use the language, scan Esperanto magazines, listen to foreign visitors, and so on, the non-Esperantist public can see a diversity of somewhat disorganized activity, involving everything from the organization of a press campaign or a public lecture series, to the inauguration of a Zamenhof Street, the performance of a play, the presentation of an exhibition, or the showing of a film about a conference.

This is, however, only the outward aspect of a much deeper cultural life. The culture that Esperantism carries with it derives from a single fundamental social and psychological fact: when thousands of people with different languages and cultures freely decide to speak the same language, there emerges a new type of society, perhaps still embryonic, an "Esperantist people" with a specific identity. While they do not forget or put aside their native cultures, they are conscious of other cultures and accordingly understand the relativity of their own. Although Esperantists differ among themselves on philosophical, political, artistic, and other opinions—much like other people, who remain largely conditioned by the society in which they live—nevertheless Esperanto allows them the opportunity to inform themselves directly and to make person-to-person contacts, and this creates a strong sense of tolerance. For this reason twentieth-century dictators have feared, correctly, that the language would emancipate people from official dogmas, and have forbidden it.

Contact and communication are the strongest characteristics of Esperantist activities. Among the Esperantists, correspondence was the first means of communication. It allows communication among both individuals and groups: "letter evenings" remain a traditional activity in many Esperanto groups. People wishing to correspond make contact with one another through magazine advertisements under the traditional rubric "Correspondents Sought" or through the Worldwide Correspondence Service operated by UEA. As for personal contacts, the Boulogne congress began a long series of international meetings. The congresses of UEA (the world congresses) and SAT are accompanied by extensive cultural and artistic activity: lectures, excursions, children's meetings, plays, puppet theater, variety performances, music, singing, artistic competitions, and so on. University courses and lectures, either in the context of congresses or as separate activities, are addressed specifically to students and scholars in various fields. Such institutions as *Geonkloj esperantistaj* (Esperantist Aunts and Uncles), the *Kastora klubo* (Beaver Club), and *Infanoj cirkaŭ la mondo* (Children around the World) encourage children to learn Esperanto and work for its dissemination. The *Pasporta servo* (Passport Service) of the youth organization TEJO, already mentioned, facilitates international travel, particularly for young people, through the assistance of hospitable Esperantists across the world. Attractive places to meet other speakers of the language are provided by the cultural centers, a unique institution in the Esperanto movement, which combine vacations with various levels of Esperanto courses. Among these centers are the Esperantist Cultural Center in La Chaux-de-Fonds, Switzerland, the Château Grésillon in Baugé, France, the International Esperanto Teaching Center in Pisanica, Bulgaria, and other occasional summer meeting places, in which Esperantists from throughout the world learn and relax in a friendly atmosphere. Esperanto's achievements in promoting international communication and educating all people about the treasures of human thought can be observed in several impressive Esperanto museums—in Vienna, Gray (France), Sant Pau D'Ordal (Spain), and elsewhere—and in several libraries, all of which oblige the objective visitor to acknowledge the communicative value and the success of Esperanto.

The circulation and exchange of ideas and information within the Esperanto movement takes place regularly through a kind of irrigation network of magazines and journals, a rich and diverse group that includes over two hundred titles, broadly divisible into four groups: (1) magazines and journals about Esperanto, (2) specialized scientific, literary, and cultural journals, (3) magazines on political, religious, and philosophical topics, and (4) national magazines designed to inform Esperantists about a given country. Because this last category of magazines often receives financial support from the governments in question, they are among the best technically. Outstanding among them are _La espero_ (Republic of Korea) and _El popola Ĉinio_ (People's Republic of China), which are interesting to read because of the high quality of their contents and also convincing examples of Esperanto journalism for skeptics beyond the Esperanto movement. Magazines without such subsidy nevertheless constitute some 98 percent of all magazines published in Esperanto. Because every national, regional, and sometimes local, association has its publication, we find great diversity in content and format. Many reach an international public because of their high quality, regular publication, and attractive appearance. _Heroldo de Esperanto_, with news from the entire Esperantist world, is the most frequently published Esperanto periodical, and also includes occasional scientific or travel supplements in its slightly old-fashioned newspaper format. The journals of the Universal Esperanto Association, _Esperanto_, and its youth section TEJO, _Kontakto_, have a style of presentation best described as classic contemporary. _Sennaciulo_, of SAT, shows by its appearance that it takes its philosophy seriously, while _Paco_ (Peace) achieves an almost bourgeois respectability. _La kancerkliniko_ (The Cancer Clinic), a satirical magazine, is among the most entertaining. We could cite many other periodicals—literary (_Fonto, Literatura foiro_), on popular science and culture (_Sennacieca revuo, Kulturaj kajeroj_), scholarly (_Medicina internacia revuo, Matematiko translimen, Tutmondaj sciencoj kaj teknikoj, Internacia pedagogia revuo_), and numerous others. Among the more recent additions, _Monato_ introduced a new style of journalism in Esperanto when it began publication a dozen years ago. It follows the format and contents of the well-known newsmagazines of Europe and America, offering news and commentary on political, economic, and other world events. This is the first time that current events at the national and international level have been surveyed from month to month in Esperanto. Side by side with magazines for professional communication and for entertainment, *Monato* owes its success to Esperantists' interest in current happenings in the world beyond Esperanto.

On the airwaves, thirteen radio stations in twelve countries broadcast in Esperanto, including stations in Warsaw, the Vatican, Beijing, and Zagreb. In 1990, 5,329 broadcasts totaled 2,072 hours.

ESPERANTO AND EDUCATION

The activities mentioned so far are aimed at people already integrated to some degree into the Esperanto-speaking community. Naturally, it is through teaching the language that this community expands. For this reason, Esperanto speakers have always attached great importance to the teaching of their language, and their ranks include many teachers, amateur and professional. These teachers must deal with a diverse learning public, for whom they have generally adapted their teaching methods well and among whom they have carried out various classroom experiments on the learnability of Esperanto. This public comes from many social levels and extends from preschool classes (native speakers of Esperanto are rare, but a few parents teach Esperanto to their children) to retirement age, when greater leisure time encourages learning. Instruction may take place as an official part of the curriculum in some schools, or through individual initiatives in evening courses, after-class programs, weekend courses, or vacation courses. Because such courses are generally not compulsory and the students most frequently adults, in-school programs work smoothly and other courses reach a higher cultural level than is customary in the social group in question.

There are more than 2,100 Esperanto textbooks in over fifty languages. Esperanto pedagogy is discussed in professional papers and often runs ahead of pedagogy for other languages by several decades, as the example of Andreo Cseh reveals. In 1929 Cseh invented the direct method of language instruction. The diversity of the public provides a convenient field for pedagogical experiments. In this regard outstanding work continues to be done by the Esperanto Department of the University of Budapest, and by the Institute of Cybernetics at Paderborn, Germany, under the leadership of Helmar Frank, a specialist in computer-assisted instruction. At the University of Illinois, Bruce Sherwood led an effort to develop instructional systems for computers and for teaching by telephone. The computer project Distributed Language Translation (DLT), launched in 1985 by the Dutch firm BSO, of Utrecht, under the direction of Toon Witkam, employs a somewhat modified Esperanto as a computer interlanguage ("black-box language") to reduce the number of channels in multilingual, computer-assisted translation.[3] Its efforts may well lead to an increase in the popularity of Esperanto in scientific circles. Undoubtedly the introduction of Esperanto into Chinese higher educational institutions as an optional field (1983) will lead to significant innovation in teaching methods. The interest of physicists and mathematicians in the teaching of Esperanto shows that we are shifting from empirical to scientific approaches for teaching the language. In fact, Esperanto is an ideal language for experiment, since its logic and regularity allows its structure to be systematized easily. But the classic teaching methods also have a secure future, and the variety of students and learning conditions requires constant inventiveness and adaptability. The range of talent and experience is vast, from professional researchers at one end to willing amateurs offering evening courses at the other. Esperanto is perhaps the only field to have so many nonprofessional teachers. Yet it remains the most rapidly learned language and the language in which the average student can expect to achieve the highest level of proficiency. As early as 1933 the American educational psychologist E. L. Thorndike concluded that a year of Esperanto instruction at the college level equaled four years of instruction at that level in French or German. Two experiments carried out under the auspices of UNESCO (1973–1974, 1975–1976) with some one thousand schoolchildren from various European countries confirmed Thorndike's finding. Helmar Frank, for his part, indicates that 1500 hours of instruction are needed for a French child to reach the Baccalauréat level in English, whereas 150 are sufficient for the same competence Esperanto. This conclusion agrees with the findings of other experiments. All of them reinforce not only that Esperanto can be learned with relative ease, regardless of the student's linguistic background, but also that Esperanto helps students to learn their own languages and other foreign languages better, and increases their motivation to learn about other countries.[4]

The dissemination of Esperanto through formal, in-school instruction is still modest, but the numbers are rising steadily. In 1970 Esperanto was taught in fifteen institutions of higher education across the world; this number rose to fifty-one by 1980 and to 110 (in twenty-two countries) by 1985. The number of courses has been doubling every fifteen years. The number of universities in which Esperanto is taught increased from 30 in 1970 to 125 in 1986. In addition to the countries traditionally strong in Esperanto, such as Bulgaria, Hungary, and Poland, the list of countries with universities that teach Esperanto includes Romania, China, and the United States (Pirlot 1986).

ESPERANTO AND THE PUBLIC

The aim of Esperantism, to disseminate Esperanto as a means of international communication, inspires various points of view among the Esperantists themselves. These points of view also vary from country to country, depending on local conditions, the status of Esperanto, government language policies (for example, eastern and central European governments have been more concrete, western European governments more theoretical, in their support of Esperanto), and, finally, on the motives of the Esperantists themselves: some insist on the Internal Idea and hence their activity has a more philosophical cast, while others insist on the need to treat Esperanto objectively and neutrally like any other language. Still others emphasize that belonging to a voluntary linguistic minority produces a new kind of international culture, on which the Esperantist identity is based. These tendencies coexist peacefully, proving that we can look at the movement from several different standpoints. Far from fracturing its unity, these points of view combine to create a rich diversity of approaches to the language.

Despite generous patrons, the support of a few corporations that advertise in Esperanto, and, in some countries, state support, the Esperanto movement does not have at its disposal the financial resources needed to launch truly effective publicity campaigns. This lack of an economic base limits the movement to what is certainly a large and expanding, but nonetheless closed and self-supporting circle of activists. Independence and enthusiasm are certainly advantages, and they have allowed

Esperantism to live through periods of active opposition from certain political regimes.[5] Through simple moral strength the Esperantists have developed from a tiny group of individuals into the current Esperanto movement, and this is a remarkable phenomenon, particularly when compared with the huge financial resources and economic pressure whereby a few nations support their linguistic superiority.

But this noble motivating force, originating primarily in idealism, has its limiting aspect, because independence heroically achieved can lead to a certain closedness, a separateness with respect to the outside world. The constant struggles of the Esperantists over an entire century, against lack of interest, opposition (most often irrational opposition), misinformation and pseudoinformation, have left them with no illusions, and have given them a certain clarity of vision and a strong awareness of their cultural uniqueness and membership in an intellectual elite. Accordingly they tend to isolate themselves by retiring into their own world, or they prefer individual initiatives to large-scale, carefully planned activity. Because they know that so far their cause has progressed as a result of grassroots action by dedicated individuals, and not because of the support of official authorities, they prefer to persuade individuals individually. Thus Esperanto progresses from person to person more often than from group to group. The advantage of this process lies in the fact that interpersonal contact carries great persuasive force, and accordingly the new recruit remains strongly tied to the recruiter. But this mode of dissemination works slowly. Fortunately it is associated with other approaches. Exploiting its size and prestige, the Universal Esperanto Association has long been active with intergovernmental organizations. In 1954 it presented a petition signed by 492 organizations with 15,454,780 members and bearing the signatures of a further 895,432 individuals. As a result of this petition, UNESCO became aware of the strength of the Esperanto movement and, in a resolution of the General Conference that met in Montevideo in 1954, it requested the director general to collaborate with UEA on matters of common interest. UNESCO established consultative relations (category B) with UEA. A further resolution in support of Esperanto was approved by the General Conference in 1985. Calling for recognition of the centennial of Esperanto in 1987, it began the process whereby the Esperanto movement mobilized all its members at all levels and in every country to use this anniversary as a way of bringing its message to the public.

Over the years, this message has changed somewhat; it now puts greater stress on the practical and objectively observable aspects of the international language. It points out the economic potential of Esperanto, particularly in the area of translation and interpretation. On the basis of the positive experience acquired from congress to congress (and the world congresses are numerically among the largest international gatherings), it shows that communication in Esperanto flows easily (and without cost) among people from many different nations. It also emphasizes the advantages of a neutral language in sustaining minority languages, which might thereby preserve their identity in the face of the cultural domination of major languages or the linguistic hegemony of the great powers. Finally, it proposes the only simple way in which all participants in multilingual international meetings can express themselves and make themselves understood on the basis of linguistic equality.

But the non-Esperantist public is still unaware of the problems arising from linguistic diversity, and of the huge loss of time, money, and energy involved. The unsatisfactory results of the teaching of national languages, despite expensive equipment and instruction, will perhaps cause students and teachers to dream, as Leibnitz and Komensky dreamed, of a rational and easy universal language. Although such a language has never been more necessary than now, few people declare themselves ready to learn the only such language that has been functioning, perfectly and visibly, for the past century. Even among the many people sympathetic to the cause of Esperanto, who support it in theory and in principle, relatively few take the step of actually learning the language. Concrete profit would probably provide the most powerful attraction. In the countries of western Europe, · more than 80 percent of the high school students are encouraged to learn English (often vainly), not for its cultural value, but because English is regarded, often erroneously, as synonymous with professional success and upward mobility. Esperanto could perform this role of international communication more effectively, and with greater profit to more young people, than any national language. Unfortunately it still is not serving this function because many barriers stand in the way of its general adoption.

These obstacles are primarily political, social, and psychological. On the political front, the current major powers are
firmly committed to a policy of linguistic domination, although
inevitably such hegemony declines as economic fortunes decline.
In the area of social concerns, those in charge seem to fear that a
common language could unite their charges: all kinds of language
specialists defend Babel because in Babel consists the prosperity
of their profession; and in various countries the intellectual elites,
union leaders, even religious leaders, oppose a common means of
communication because it would lead to the loss of much of their
power and prestige. Psychological opposition comes from a
subconscious resistance, unreachable by rational argument
precisely because it originates in irrational psychic impulses.
The pseudo-rational arguments, repeated time and again by those
opposed to Esperanto—artificiality, unnaturalness, cold logi-
cality, lack of poetry, oddness, and so on—barely mask their lack
of objectivity, since one cannot judge Esperanto objectively
without knowing something about it, which is exactly what they
seek to prevent.[6]

However, Esperanto does indeed have its irrational aspects,
though they are not to be found in any of its linguistic characteristics. In many cases the motives for learning it are no more
rational than the motives of those opposing it. Idealism derived
from the Internal Idea has a positive effect on the evolution of
humanity, but it is as much an emotive as a rational response to
the language problem. Although many scholars tend to reduce
Esperanto to a mere language and empty it of all ideological
and emotional implications, it cannot be entirely separated
from the ancient ideal of a linguistically and spiritually united
humankind. Despite its perfect suitability for objective neutral
communication, or perhaps precisely because of it, Esperanto
continues to symbolize the idea of world understanding and a
universal order. While the ethnic languages point to confusion,
chaos, and the separation of humankind, and while the other
planned languages themselves enter a kind of artificial Babel
because they lack their own cohesive ideal, Esperanto continues
to call for world unity to solve world problems. Even if the
various nations should one day choose a common planned language other than Esperanto, that language will survive only as
long as people dream of unity and peace.

Esperanto has become the language of an Esperantist diaspora. Esperanto culture flourishes, undeniably and irresistibly, with or without official recognition. Even if the entire Esperanto movement were to disappear, it has lived long enough to create an independent culture worthy of specific study. What is more, such a disappearance is purely theoretical: despite the obstacles that we have mentioned, the activities of the Esperanto movement seem to be bringing increasing success. They appear to guarantee the constant and sustained dissemination of the international language.

Chapter 7

Conclusion

"All theoretical argument is beside the point: Esperanto already works," affirmed the well-known linguist Antoine Meillet in 1928. Hundreds of thousands of Esperantists have proved him right. Anonymous students in night classes or scholars of world repute, together they have vitalized the movement through their dedication and idealism. Over the past century the idea and project of a single idealistic individual, Lazar Ludwik Zamenhof, has extended across the continents as a multifaceted, pluralistic, but united diaspora, a harbinger of that world order of which Zamenhof dreamed. Unlike other planned languages, Esperanto emerged from its intellectual and social birthplace and established itself among the modest but hardworking and thoughtful elements of society that have defended it obstinately and generously over the years.

Why did Esperanto gain this popular support when other projects remained closed in on themselves? Because it was at once both a language and a message. Its very name, Esperanto, which soon replaced the original name, Lingvo Internacia, associates it with the conscious and unconscious hopes of humanity. This double nature, as language and symbol, carries with it both opportunity and risk: opportunity because it is capable of serving as a unifying factor, a role that is denied both to the ethnic languages, too closely linked with national identities and systems, and to the other planned languages, which have so far failed to eclipse it with their merely linguistic qualities; and risk because the ideological implications attract some but repel others and can create confusion about its real aim. For this reason many users of Esperanto distinguish between Esperanto and Esperantism, which they define as a doctrine based on the Internal Idea, while they regard Esperanto as a strictly neutral means of communication usable for all purposes.

It is enough to observe it to see that Esperanto works. Anyone who in fact observes how economically advantageous it can be, compared with the national languages, can only wish for its introduction as soon as possible in all schools where competent teachers are available—and can only welcome the increasingly frequent educational experiments on Esperanto being pursued in various countries. When we look at the relative ease of communication and the precision of Esperanto and consider the cost of language services in international conferences, we can only wonder that the superiority of Esperanto has yet to be brought home to its potential users. We can only wonder at the fact that its educational value is disregarded by the very people who note the relative failure of language instruction in the schools and its negative consequences in large parts of society; we can only wonder, finally (though there are many other wonders), at the fact that the cultural, social, and educational role of Esperanto is so misrepresented or little understood by cultural and educational professionals.

This neglect of the obvious shows that the satisfactory functioning of Esperanto is not enough to guarantee its dissemination. Its dissemination depends also on psychological, social, and political factors, which vary from country to country and social level to social level. Will its progress continue? If we look back at its hundred-year history, we realize that this history is simply the latest stage in a longer evolutionary process, growing in strength since the sixteenth century, and gaining speed with the increasing consciousness that we are all citizens of the world and members of a united humanity. Because an international language can only contribute positively to this trend, Esperantism has expanded steadily, unextinguished by the death of its creator and by two world wars. At each setback it has revived, and even in those countries where it was forbidden it has regained its lost ground. This suggests that it has incorporated the evolutionary tendencies of the day on such matters as communication problems and linguistic needs to a degree sufficient to attract new users and to guarantee the success of its strategies.

Many signs point to a growing vitality. Within the Esperanto movement, literary and artistic activity, translation, education, professional application, the modernization and versatility of the Esperanto press, the use of Esperanto as an experimental language in computers and elsewhere—all are the more remarkable if we consider that the number of dues-paying members is increasing relatively slowly. In fact, in eastern and central Europe there has been a marked diminution in membership in national associations over the past couple of years, as people have found that they can use Esperanto for international contacts without having to join an organization; but at the same time the very relaxation of organizational discipline has opened new opportunities for travel and literary expression. It is significant and promising that Esperanto is no longer a purely European initiative: active associations in Japan, Vietnam, Korea, China, Iran, Madagascar, Zaire, and various parts of South America have widened the prospects for the future considerably.

Outside the movement, Esperanto may profit from circumstances favoring an international language. The need for rapid and frequent worldwide communication reflects a growing trend toward unity and cooperation. Esperantists must bring pressure to bear, in every possible way, on the European Parliament, since as the European Community is transformed into an authentic political federation, with ten or a dozen major languages, Esperanto will be afforded a unique chance unavailable in other parts of the world. For the same reason they should join the battle, alongside the countries of the third world, for those countries' linguistic independence. The linguistic imperialism of a few major powers has denied most nations their own adequate means of expression, forcing English and French on them, along with their respective cultures. If the third world wishes to acquire linguistic independence and also communicate with the world, it needs a language at least as international in character as the languages of the former colonists. That language could be Esperanto.

The essential message of Esperanto is that an international language should belong to everyone, and not only a few privileged people, nations, or sections of the population. Its very conception implies the denial of elitism, hegemony, and all forms of dominance by the few over the many. Esperanto has been called the Latin of modern democracy because people need a common language to become and remain free. It is already apparent, wherever Esperanto is used, that it serves not only as a means of communication, but also as a means of opening new avenues for information, contacts, exchanges—in short, as a way of achieving a more rational, aware and comprehensive culture and society. Herein lies its unique educational value. The fact that, among all previous and subsequent projects, Esperanto alone became a living language, spoken by more people than 95 percent of the known languages of the world, is an arresting linguistic fact, making Esperanto unique among planned languages.[1] On the other hand, Esperanto stands apart from the ethnic languages in that it alone is capable of fully performing the role of an international language: a given national language will not lose its specifically national characteristics (phonology, structure, logic) just because it is used as an interlanguage among people of different nationalities. If we understand that internationality is not limited to contacts among the few (for example, in professional or business circles, or among a few peoples or areas), and if we define internationality in its universal sense, then we are forced to acknowledge that all ethnic languages remain essentially national, based on national cultures, while Esperanto is essentially universal.

The dream that everyone might learn this language side by side with his or her native language is, then, a serious dream. If it is to be realized, the Esperantists must do more to coordinate their forces. They must inform the public more systematically, using modern methods to do so. They must extend their influence into all technologies, as they are already doing in informatics: they must gain political support, and they must strengthen their financial base. But the success of the language does not depend only on the Esperantists. Modern sales campaigns and advertising are expensive for what is essentially a popular movement. Precisely because of the social origins and situation of Esperantism, Esperantists are lacking among the decision makers and economic leaders, who prefer to use the languages of the most influential major powers. Among these powers are not only national governments, but also financial, economic, and ideological forces. If the ideal of the Esperantists is to be realized, these powers will have to retreat from their ambitions of hegemony, cease forcing their languages on others, and examine the language problem objectively and unselfishly. Despite the positive declarations of a few official authorities, it seems likely that a rational and responsible approach to this problem is still a long way off, although the world communication situation, the development of various countries and sections of the population, the spread of education—in sum, everything that we call progress—makes Esperanto more and more necessary.

Notes

INTRODUCTION

1. While the adjective *interlinguistic* was used by George Meredith as early as 1879, the term *interlinguistics* first appears in the early years of this century. Stojan 1929 records the publication of *The International Language: A Journal of Interlinguistics* in London from 1911 to 1915. Jespersen's classic definition of the term appears in an essay entitled "Interlinguistics" in a small volume published in 1931 (see Jespersen 1962 for the text). Tonkin 1977 lists three definitions of the term: (1) "the study of the linguistic elements necessary to the formation of a constructed international language" (and, we should add, the comparative study of projects for a constructed international language), (2) "the comparative study of widely known languages to determine which elements are common to a number of them" (Pei and Gaynor 1969), and (3) "the study of the social, cultural and linguistic conditions necessary for the acceptance of a constructed international language." See also Schubert and Maxwell 1988 and Haupenthal 1966 for more extensive material on the study of interlinguistics. Gilbert 1962 and Blanke 1982 are also helpful. On scholarly responses to interlinguistics, see Gotoo 1986.

2. We have translated *planlingvo* as "planned language" throughout. The English term is not wholly satisfactory, because rather too specific. On the problem of terminology see Blanke 1987. For the terminology of interlinguistics in general see also Pei 1965 and Mounin 1958.

CHAPTER 1

1. The classic survey of international language projects is Couturat and Leau 1903 and 1907. See also Drezen 1931a, Blanke 1985, and the best English-language overview, Large 1985. Knowlson 1975 examines

"philosophical" language projects in England and France, Murray Cohen 1977 pays particular attention to England, and Strasser 1988 examines the connection between such projects and cryptography. See also Jonathan Cohen 1954, Salmon 1966 and 1979, and Slaughter 1982.

2. René Descartes, *Oeuvres et lettres* (Paris: NRF, 1953), pp. 911–15.

3. G. W. Leibniz, *Opera omnia* (Geneva, 1768), pp. 7–8.

4. On Dalgarno see the chapter in Shumaker 1982.

5. *Pasigraphie ou premiers elements du nouvel art-science d'écrire et d'imprimer en une langue de manière à être lu et entendu dans toute autre langue sans traduction.* The term *pasigraphy* is first recorded in English in 1796, in the *Monthly Review* 19: 357.

6. On early attempts to simplify Latin, see Couturat and Leau 1903, Drezen 1931a, and Strasser 1986.

7. Blanke 1985:335–37 offers a useful bibliography on Volapük, and Haupenthal's edition (1982) of Schleyer 1880 includes a full bibliography. See also Haupenthal 1985. Discussions of Volapük in English are sparse, but see Large 1985:64–71, and Golden 1987.

8. On the value of Esperanto as a subject of scholarly study, and the relative lack of attention devoted to it, see Edwards 1986, Dasgupta 1987b, and Dulichenko 1988.

CHAPTER 2

1. An area containing parts of what are now Lithuania, northeastern Poland, Belarus, and Ukraine.

2. *OV* 417–18; *Let* 1:343–44. Translation in Boulton 1960:6–7.

3. Letter to Michaux, 21 February 1905. *Let* 1:107.

4. Biographies of Zamenhof include Boulton 1960, the standard English-language biography, and Maimon 1978 (in Esperanto), which offers interesting insight into the social and cultural background of Zamenhof. Gold 1987 offers some useful correctives to Maimon. See also Lieberman 1979, Berdichevsky 1986. Heller 1985 is a biography of Zamenhof's daughter Lidia.

5. The allusion is to Zamenhof's poem *La Espero* (Hope), which has become the anthem of the Esperantists: *En la mondon venis nova sento; / Tra la mondo iras forta voko. / Per flugiloj de facila vento / Nun de loko*

flugas ĝi al loko. 'Into the world has come a new feeling; through the world goes a powerful call. On wings of easy wind it now flies from place to place'.

6. The tragic history of Nazi and Stalinist persecutions is told in Lins 1988a and 1988b. Sadler and Lins 1972 offer a briefer account in English.

7. Zamenhof particularly likes the expression *Esperantujo* 'the land or realm of Esperanto' to denote the community of Esperantists. He also sometimes alludes to *la popolo esperantista,* 'the Esperantist people'. Such analogical vocabulary suggests that, for him, Esperantism constitutes a true society, a shadow of the society to come. [PJ]

8. The Esperanto flag was created in 1905 on the eve of the Boulogne congress by the local Esperanto group. The flag is green with a green star on a white background in the top right-hand corner. See Kökeny and Bleier 1933:501. [PJ]

9. The contribution of the Universal Esperanto Association to world peace is described by Lins 1986. On sociological aspects of Esperanto, see Forster 1982, Wood 1979, Jordan 1987, Isaev 1981.

10. On the history of Esperanto in intergovernmental organizations, see Lapenna, Lins, and Carlevaro 1974, Lapenna 1970–1971, Tonkin 1982, and Harry and Mandel 1979. UEA 1983 deals specifically with UNESCO, and Sekelj 1981 with the nonaligned movement. On language in intergovernmental organizations generally, see also Humblet 1984 and Piron and Tonkin 1979.

CHAPTER 3

1. The translation is based on the English version of the *Fundamento* (1905), with some excisions (including examples of many of the rules). For the full text, see Zamenhof 1905 (1963):57–61. Adequate grammatical descriptions of Esperanto are still sadly lacking. Wells 1978 is the nearest approach. See also Kalocsay and Waringhien 1980, Duc Goninaz 1987a, Mattos 1987a and 1987b. Lo Jacomo 1981 deals particularly with language change.

2. Among the attempts to break out of this terminological and conceptual straitjacket are those of Piron 1981 and Auld 1965, the latter in his English-language textbook. See also note 4, below.

3. It would be naive to suppose that internationality consists primarily in the greatest diversity of lexical sources. A language com-

prised of words from all languages would be statistically but not linguistically international. The proportion of each language in the whole would be so small that the sum of such contributions would seem foreign to everyone. It has been calculated that we can understand 80 percent of a language by means of only two thousand words. If we were to choose, say, one hundred languages (thereby eliminating 96 percent of the spoken languages of the world), the share of any one would be twenty words. What would be the advantage of that? Such a language would be difficult to memorize, whereas Esperanto is easy for many people to memorize. [PJ] On the sources of Esperanto, see Gregor 1982, Mattos 1987a. On the etymology see also Szerdahelyi 1987. Duc Goninaz 1974 and Kolker 1987 consider specifically Russian influences, and Golden 1980a, 1980b, and 1985 looks at the influence of other planned languages on Zamenhof. Gold 1980 and 1982 explores Hebrew and Yiddish influences. Blanke 1981 offers a comparison with German. On the larger question of the typological classification of Esperanto, see Wells 1978, Balbin 1987, Duc Goninaz 1987a, and, especially, Piron 1981.

4. English employs many words both as verbs and nouns, and nominal forms in English can, of course, readily serve as adjectives. Cf. Zamenhof's observation in a letter of 24 February 1907 regarding the Esperanto verb *stampi* (*OV* 538–39). [PJ] The question of the "grammatical character of roots" has been a subject of considerable controversy among Esperanto experts over the years. The classic statement on the subject is Kalocsay 1938, but in recent years his theories have been questioned by Szerdahelyi 1976b and others, who criticize what they perceive as Kalocsay's tendency to apply to Esperanto categories derived from other languages. For references see Tonkin 1977:17 and Haupenthal 1968. See also Kalocsay and Waringhien 1980:374–85, Mattos 1987c, Reiersøl and Marble 1949, Reiersøl and Wood 1987, Dasgupta 1987a, Rokicki 1987.

5. Passive participles were the subject of intense debate among language specialists in the 1950s and 1960s. See especially Kalocsay 1966. At the heart of this debate were sets of assumptions about the aspectual nature of the Esperanto verb discerned in the language by speakers of Romance and Slavic languages and denied by speakers of Germanic languages. The Academy of Esperanto decided in favor of the former.

6. Needless to say, in many of its details the table is largely theoretical. The essential point, made earlier, is that such transformations can be extended grammatically as far as we have lexemes to extend them: they are limited only by semantics and the ability of the audience to decode them. In practice, then, several of these combinations are rare.

The suffix *-iĝ-*, for example, tends to be subsumed by *-ig-* when the two might be expected to appear in combination. Hence *turnigi* can signify either *igi turni* ('make to turn'; transitive) or *igi turniĝi* ('make to turn'; intransitive). Only if a speaker felt the necessity of indicating that the second meaning was intended (and generally the context leaves little doubt) might the two suffixes appear together.

7. On the origins of this usage in Slavic languages, see Duc Goninaz 1974.

8. Sherwood 1982a offers a more skeptical view.

9. See Wells 1978:39–42 for a brief and clear explanation of word order in Esperanto.

10. For a more detailed discussion, see Janton 1987.

CHAPTER 4

1. Work on the development of technical terms in Esperanto is coordinated by the Terminology Section of the International Esperanto Scientific Association (ISAE), based in Canada, and the Esperanto Terminology Center (TEC) in Czechoslovakia. The Center for Research and Documentation on World Language Problems organizes conferences and coordinates research on international aspects of language problems. Its journal, *Language Problems and Language Planning* (*LPLP*), enjoys a high scholarly reputation. It organizes annual conferences in New York in December in cooperation with the Translation Division of the United Nations, organizes an annual Conference on Esperantology, and publishes an occasional series of collected scholarly papers. A CRD bibliography of dissertations on Esperanto and interlinguistics has recently been compiled (Symoens 1989). On the work of language institutions in Esperanto see Venture 1987 and Lo Jacomo 1981. On libraries see McKown 1981.

2. For a recent view, see Ouyang Wendao and Sherwood 1986. See also Lewin and Jordan 1981. An international conference on science and technology in Esperanto now takes place biennially in China, attracting scientists from around the world, and the Chinese Academy of Sciences publishes a journal, *Tutmondaj sciencoj kaj teknikoj*. The work of the International Academy of Sciences of San Marino, which offers university-level instruction on a range of subjects in Esperanto in sessions held in various locations in Europe and beyond, helps to expand scientific and scholarly vocabulary and to make scientific discourse in Esperanto more widely familiar.

3. The passage, from the sequence *Ahasvero de amo* (written in 1923), is extraordinarily difficult to translate. The lines in question read, *Hararo via estas trankvile onda maro. / Ne taŭzis la supraĵon ankoraŭ kisomevoj.* 'Your hair is a quietly undulating sea'. The surface is variously ruffled by seagulls or by kisses, depending on whether the tenor or the vehicle (to use the terms of I. A. Richards) is intended. The poem appears in Kalocsay's *Streĉita kordo* (Budapest: Literatura Mondo, 1931), whose publication decisively influenced the subsequent development of Esperanto poetry.

4. *Literatura Foiro* 69 (October 1981): 1.

5. The *Kalevala* was translated by J. E. Leppäkoski (2d ed. Helsinki: Esperanto-Asocio de Finnlando, 1985). *Infero*, Kálmán Kalocsay's translation of the *Inferno* (1933; 2d ed. La Chaux-de-Fonds/Milano: Literatura Foiro, 1979), is widely regarded as a classic of the art of Esperanto translation. The complete *Divine Comedy* has also been translated by Giovanni Peterlongo as *Dia komedio* (2d ed. Milano: SIEI, 1979). On Shakespeare, see Boulton 1987. Translations of eighteen Shakespeare plays have been published, some in more than one version. They begin with Zamenhof's translation of *Hamlet* (1894) and include impressive renderings of *King Lear* by Kálmán Kalocsay, *Othello* by Reto Rossetti, and *Twelfth Night* by William Auld.

CHAPTER 5

1. The translation of Andersen was published in four volumes after Zamenhof's death, over a protracted period (1923, 1926, 1932, 1963). The complete translation of the Old Testament was ultimately published in 1926 in London by the British and Foreign Bible Society, but the earliest sections appeared in 1911 and subsequent years. A collected edition of Andersen has recently (1990) appeared in Japan.

2. The debate over neologisms is as old as Esperanto itself. Some, such as the teacher Andreo Cseh, have argued for simplicity, stressing the role of Esperanto as an easy-to-learn auxiliary language. Others have argued against the introduction of too many new, largely European, roots, since this might compromise the internationality of the language. Piron 1986b is a leading advocate for this position, arguing for exploitation of the full potential of Esperanto through compounds rather than neologisms. Waringhien 1959:244–56 favors gradual expansion in line with the natural evolution of the language. Rumler 1986 and 1987 makes the case for a multiplicity of styles in Esperanto and hence the need for abundant, even redundant, synonyms. See also Kock 1987a. Vatré 1987 provides a glossary of neologisms. The debate over neologisms is really

only one manifestation of the tension between schematism and naturalism evident in Esperanto from the beginning and leading to the Ido schism of 1907–1908.

3. Richardson 1988 touches briefly on Esperanto literature, but there is no extensive treatment in English other than Hagler's dissertation (1971). See, however, Verloren van Themaat 1972 and Tonkin and Hoeksema 1982 on translation, and Auld 1976 on poetry. Studies in Esperanto include Auld 1979 and Benczik 1980. Pechan 1979 provides a literary survey. Auld 1984 offers an extensive anthology of original poetry, and Auld 1991 provides a representative anthology of poetry and prose, original and translated. On the writing of poetry in Esperanto, see Kalocsay, Waringhien, and Bernard 1968 and Ragnarsson 1988. On the novel see Auld 1981. Rossetti and Vatré 1990 provide a two-volume anthology of short stories by various authors.

4. The periodization is Auld's (1984; see his introduction), derived from an earlier version of his anthology (1960).

5. See the anthologies of short stories edited by Rossetti and Szilágyi 1964 and Rossetti and Vatré 1990.

6. On Régulo's contribution see Kock 1987b, Benczik 1987, and the massive festschrift for Régulo, *Serta* 1987.

7. Delaire 1964:xv.

8. There is a large and growing popular musical culture in Esperanto, with records and cassettes appearing in increasing numbers and performing groups working the circuit of Esperanto conferences and events.

9. The Universal Esperanto Association publishes a 400-page catalogue of books in stock, and several national Esperanto associations, including those in the United States and Britain, run mail-order book services. Esperanto books are unfortunately seldom available in bookstores.

CHAPTER 6

1. The figure of 120,000 was arrived at by adding up the declared membership of national and international Esperanto associations, several of which (including some of the largest) were omitted because they do not publish their membership numbers. Membership of local organizations would of course be larger. Although membership numbers for the Universal Esperanto Association remain at a little over 40,000,

reports from China and certain other countries indicate that well over a quarter of a million people are learning Esperanto at any one time. On UEA and other international Esperanto associations, see Richardson 1988:45–56, Forster 1982, Wood 1979, and UEA 1991.

2. See Saletti 1986.

3. Witkam 1983 explains the basis of the DLT project. Schubert 1988 and Sadler 1991 provide updates. See also Schubert 1987, Hutchins 1986:287–91, Neijt 1986.

4. On arguments for the teaching of Esperanto, see Sherwood 1983, Tonkin and Leon-Smith 1979, Piron 1986a, Chiti-Batelli 1988, Gregor 1979, and the references in Tonkin 1977:35–36. On Thorndike's work see Thorndike 1933 and Blanke 1985:170–71. See also Maxwell 1988.

5. See Lins 1988a and 1988b, Sadler and Lins 1972. The process of democratization in the former Soviet Union has led to the publication of several studies drawing on previously unavailable archival material relating to the Great Purges of the 1930s. We can expect more to follow.

6. On psychological and social resistance to Esperanto, see Piron 1982, 1987b, 1987c, and 1988, Forster 1987, Janton 1983. Cf. Edwards and MacPherson 1987.

CHAPTER 7

1. Only 163 of the three thousand or so known spoken languages in 1980 had more than one million speakers. [PJ]

Bibliography

All works cited in the text and a few additional items are included in the bibliography, which does not pretend to completeness. Fuller information on linguistic studies of Esperanto can be obtained in Wood 1982, and Ockey 1982 provides a bibliography of dictionaries. Tonkin 1977 offers a general introduction to the field of Esperanto and language problems. Probably the best source of information on current publications is the annual bibliography of the Modern Language Association (Tonkin, Edwards, and Verloren van Themaat 1979–). This listing runs to several hundred items each year, in all languages.

The sources mentioned above are all in English. The reader of Esperanto will find Haupenthal 1966 useful, especially on classic texts in Esperanto and interlinguistics. Readers of German will find a full bibliography in Blanke 1985. Stojan 1929 provides exhaustive coverage of the early period and is accessible for the English speaker.

Reference works in Esperanto include the Esperanto Encyclopedia (Kökeny and Bleier 1933), the Yearbook of UEA (UEA 1991), and Waringhien's dictionary (Waringhien 1970). McKown 1981 gives information on library holdings.

For the student without extensive background, Richardson 1988 is probably the best place to start. This book also contains a short course in Esperanto and a brief dictionary. See also the popular articles by Fallows 1986, Staggs 1987, Shenker 1987, and Lee and Shapiro 1987. Eichholz and Eichholz 1982 offer a useful collection of articles and studies, intended for the general reader, on Esperanto and language problems in general. See also Forster 1982 and Tonkin 1977.

Several of the books and articles on Esperanto deal with language problems in general—for example, the early chapters of

143

Richardson 1988. The reader interested in language problems and the rationale for Esperanto might also consult Pei 1958 and 1969, Sapir 1961, and Eichholz and Eichholz 1982. English-language contributions to this topic also include Tonkin 1979a and 1979b and Piron 1979. Lewin and Jordan 1981, Sherwood 1983, and Large 1985 deal particularly with science. Readers of Italian might also consult Chiti-Batelli 1987a and 1987b and Corsetti 1976.

Albault, André. 1987. "La Akademio de Esperanto: Starigo kaj esenca rolo." In *Serta* 1987:21–36.

Auld, William. 1965. *Esperanto: A New Approach*. Brussels: Heroldo de Esperanto.

———. 1976. *The Development of Poetic Language in Esperanto*. Esperanto Documents 4A. Rotterdam: Universal Esperanto Association.

———. 1979. *Enkonduko en la originalan literaturon de Esperanto*. Saarbrücken: Artur E. Iltis.

———. 1981. *Vereco distro stilo: Romanoj en Esperanto*. Saarbrücken: Artur E. Iltis.

———. 1987. "Kulturbazo historia de la Esperanto-movado." In *Serta* 1987:43–50.

———. 1988. *La fenomeno Esperanto*. Rotterdam: Universala Esperanto-Asocio.

———. ed. 1984. *Esperanta antologio: Poemoj 1887–1981*. Rotterdam: Universala Esperanto-Asocio.

———. ed. 1991. *Nova Esperanta krestomatio*. Rotterdam: Universala Esperanto-Asocio.

Balbin, Julius. 1987. "Is Esperanto a Romance Language?" In *Geolinguistic Perspectives*, edited by Jesse Levitt, Leonard R. N. Ashley, and Kenneth H. Rogers, pp. 85–103. Lanham: University Press of America.

Benczik, Vilmos. 1980. *Studoj pri la Esperanta literaturo*. Takasago, Japan: La Kritikanto.

———. 1987. "La rolo de la eldonejo Stafeto en la konservado de la kontinueco de la Esperanta literaturo." In *Serta* 1987:61–64.

Berdichevsky, Norman. 1986. "Zamenhof and Esperanto." *Ariel* (Summer): 58–71.

Bernard, Roger. 1987. "Esperantaj kabaretoj." In *Serta* 1987:65–87.

Blanke, Detlev. 1981. *Plansprache und Nationalsprache.* Linguistische Studien 85, Reihe A. Arbeitsberichte. Berlin: Akademie der Wissenschaften der DDR, Zentralinstitut für Sprachwissenschaft.

——. 1982. *Esperanto und Wissenschaft: Zur Plansprachenproblematik.* Berlin: Kulturbund der DDR.

——. 1985. *Internationale Plansprachen: Eine Einführung.* Berlin: Akademie-Verlag.

——. 1987. "The Term 'Planned Language'." *LPLP* 11:335–49.

Bormann, Werner. 1960. *Bona Ŝanco: 12 prelegoj pri la Internacia Lingvo kaj la sociaj sciencoj.* La Laguna, Canary Islands: Stafeto.

Boulton, Marjorie. 1960. *Zamenhof, Creator of Esperanto.* London: Routledge and Kegan Paul.

——. 1987. "La evoluado de Esperanto observita tra tradukoj de Ŝekspiraj dramoj." In Mattos 1987d:39–62.

Chiti-Batelli, Andrea. 1987a. *Communication internationale et avenir des langues et des parlers en Europe.* Nice: Presses d'Europe.

——. 1987b. *La comunicazióne internazionale tra politica e glottodidattica.* Milan: Marzorati.

——. 1988. *La politica d'insegnamento delle lingue nella Comunità Europea.* Rome: Armando.

Cohen, Jonathan. 1954. "On the Project of a Universal Character." *Mind* 63:49–63.

Cohen, Murray. 1977. *Sensible Words: Linguistic Practice in England, 1640–1785.* Baltimore: Johns Hopkins University Press.

Corsetti, Renato. 1976. *Lingua e politica: Imperialismi, identità nazionali e politiche linguistiche in Asia, Africa, America Latina.* Rome: Officina Edizioni.

Couturat, Louis, and L. Leau. 1903. *Histoire de la langue universelle.* Paris: Hachette.

——. 1907. *Les nouvelles langues internationales.* Paris: Hachette.

Dasgupta, Probal. 1987a. "Kategorioj, la fleksio, la lingvistiko kaj radikoj en Esperanto." In Mattos 1987d:63–75.

———. 1987b. "Toward a Dialogue between the Sociolinguistic Sciences and Esperanto Culture." *LPLP* 11:305–34.

Delaire, Pierre. 1964. *L'espéranto vivant.* 6th ed. Orléans: the author.

Drezen, Ernest. 1930. *Analiza historio de la Esperanto-movado.* Leipzig: EKRELO.

———. 1931a. *Historio de la mondolingvo.* Moscow. Rpt. Osaka: Pirato, 1967.

———. 1931b. *Skizoj pri teorio de Esperanto.* Rpt. Aabyhøj, Denmark: DEF, 1975.

Duc Goninaz, Michel. 1974. "Les influences slaves en espéranto." *Cahiers de linguistique, d'orientalisme et de slavistique* (Université de Provence), 3–4:31–53.

———. 1987a. "Kiel priskribi Esperanton? Problemoj metodologiaj kaj terminologiaj." In *Serta* 1987:141–49.

———. ed. 1987b. *Studoj pri la Internacia Lingvo.* Ghent: AIMAV.

Dulichenko, Aleksandr. 1988. "Esperanto: A Unique Model for General Linguistics." *LPLP* 12:148–51.

Edwards, Jane. 1986. "Esperanto and an International Research Context." In Tonkin and Johnson-Weiner 1986:97–107

Edwards, John, and Lynn MacPherson. 1987. "Views of Constructed Languages, with Special Reference to Esperanto." *LPLP* 11: 283–304.

Eichholz, Rüdiger, and Vilma Sindona Eichholz, ed. 1982. *Esperanto in the Modern World.* Bailieboro, Ontario: Esperanto Press.

Fallows, James. 1986. "Esperanto Lives." *Atlantic* (December):14–24.

Forster, Peter G. 1982. *The Esperanto Movement.* Contributions to the Sociology of Language 32. The Hague, Paris, New York: Mouton.

———. 1987. "Some Social Sources of Resistance to Esperanto." In *Serta* 1987:203–11.

Gilbert, William. 1962. *Planlingvaj problemoj.* La Laguna, Canary Islands: Stafeto. 2d ed., København: TK, 1977. First edition translated by

Duncan Charters as "Problems of Languages Planned for International Use." Ms. available from Esperanto League for North America.

Gold, David L. 1980. "Towards a Study of Possible Yiddish and Hebrew Influence on Esperanto." In *Miscellanea Interlinguistica*, edited by István Szerdahelyi, pp. 300–367. Budapest: Tankönyvkiadó.

———. 1982. "Pli pri judaj aspektoj de Esperanto." *Planlingvistiko* 1: 7–14.

———. 1987. "N. Z. Maimon's *La kaŝita vivo de Zamenhof.*" In Duc Goninaz 1987b:40–57.

Golden, Bernard. 1980a. "Bibliografiaj donitaĵoj pri eblaj planlingvaj fontoj de Esperanto." In *Miscellanea Interlinguistica*, edited by István Szerdahelyi, pp. 279–99. Budapest: Tankönyvkiadó.

———. 1980b. *The Influence of Volapük on Esperanto as Indicated by Lexical Data.* Linguistische Berichte, LB-Papier Nr. 61. Wiesbaden: Vieweg.

———. 1985. "Influo de Volapuko sur la ĝermanan komponanton de Esperanto." In *Li kaj ni: Festlibro por la 80-a naskiĝtago de Gaston Waringhien*, edited by Reinhard Haupenthal, pp. 401–13. La Laguna/Antwerp: TK/Stafeto.

———. 1987. "Conservation of the Heritage of Volapük." LPLP 11: 361–67.

Gotoo, Hitosi. 1986. "Interlingvistikaj diskutoj en la historio de lingvistiko." In Umeda 1986:157–61.

Gregor, Douglas B. 1979. *The Cultural Value of Esperanto.* Esperanto Documents 19A. Rotterdam: Universal Esperanto Association.

———. 1982. *La fontoj de Esperanto.* 2d ed. Glasgow: Kardo.

Hagler, Margaret. 1971. "The Esperanto Language as a Literary Medium." Ph.D.diss., Indiana University. *Dissertation Abstracts* 32:919A.

Harry, Ralph, and Mark Mandel. 1979. *Language Equality in International Cooperation.* Esperanto Documents 21A. Rotterdam: Universal Esperanto Association.

Haupenthal, Reinhard. 1968. *Enkonduko en la libroscirncon de Esperanto.* Nuremberg: Pickel.

———. 1985. "Johann Martin Schleyer." In *Li kaj ni: Festlibro por la 80-a naskiĝtago de Gaston Waringhien*, edited by Reinhard Haupenthal, pp. 441–60. La Laguna/Antwerp: TK/Stafeto.

———. ed. 1976. *Plansprachen: Beiträge zur Interlinguistik*. Darmstadt: Wissenschaftliche Buchgesellschaft.

Heller, Wendy. 1985. *Lidia, Daughter of Esperanto*. Oxford: George Ronald.

Humblet, Jean-E. 1984. "The Language Problem in International Organizations." *International Social Science Journal* 36:143–55.

Hutchins, W. J. 1986. *Machine Translation: Past, Present, Future*. Chichester, U.K.: Ellis Horwood; New York: Wiley.

Isaev, M. I. 1981. *Jazyk Esperanto*. Moscow: Nauka.

Janton, Pierre. 1974. *L'espéranto*. Que sais-je (series). Paris: Presses Universitaires de France. 2d ed. 1977.

———. 1983. "La résistance psychologique aux langues construites, en particulier à l'espéranto." *Actes: Journée d'étude sur l'espéranto*. Saint-Denis: Cours et études de linguistique contrastive et appliquée de Vincennes, Université de Paris VIII.

———. 1987. "Latentaj strukturaj trajtoj de la Esperanta gramatiko." In Duc Goninaz 1987b:79–90.

———. 1988. *Esperanto: Lingvo, literaturo, movado*. Rotterdam: Universala Esperanto-Asocio.

Jespersen, Otto. 1962. *Selected Writings*. London: Allen and Unwin.

Jespersen, Otto, Edward Sapir, and H. N. Shenton. 1931. *International Communication*. London: Kegan Paul.

Jordan, David K. 1987. "Esperanto and Esperantism: Symbols and Motivations in a Movement for Linguistic Equality." *LPLP* 11: 104–25.

Kalocsay, Kálmán. 1938. *La gramatika karaktero de la Esperantaj radikoj*. Budapest. Reprint Saarbrücken: Artur E. Iltis, 1980.

———. 1966. *Vojaĝo inter la tempoj*. La Laguna, Canary Islands: Stafeto.

Kalocsay, Kálmán, and Gaston Waringhien. 1980. *Plena analiza gramatiko de Esperanto*. Rotterdam: Universala Esperanto-Asocio.

Kalocsay, Kálmán, Gaston Waringhien, and Roger Bernard. 1968. *Parnasa gvidlibro*. 2d ed. Warsaw: Pola Esperanto-Asocio.

Knowlson, James. 1975. *Universal Language Schemes in England and France, 1600–1800.* Toronto: University of Toronto Press.

Kock, Edwin de. 1987a. "Principoj por la takso de neologismoj." In Mattos 1987d:76–92.

———. 1987b. "La *Regula Stafeto* kaj la originala Esperanta poezio." In *Serta* 1987:301–13.

Kökeny, L., and V. Bleier, ed. 1933. *Enciklopedio de Esperanto.* 2 vols. Budapest: Literatura Mondo. Reprint (1 vol.). Budapest: Hungara Esperanto-Asocio, 1979.

Kolker, Boris. 1987. "Kontribuo de la rusa lingvo al la verba sistemo de Esperanto." In *Serta* 1987:301–13.

Lapenna, Ivo. 1970–1971. "The Common Language Question before International Organizations." *La monda lingvo-problemo* 2: 83–102; 3:11–30.

Lapenna, Ivo, Ulrich Lins, and Tazio Carlevaro. 1974. *Esperanto en perspektivo: Faktoj kaj analizoj pri la Internacia Lingvo.* London and Rotterdam: Centro de Esploro kaj Dokumentado pri la Monda Lingvo-Problemo.

Large, Andrew. 1983. *The Foreign-Language Barrier.* London: André Deutsch.

———. 1985. *The Artificial Language Movement.* Oxford: Blackwell.

Lee, John, and Joseph P. Shapiro. 1987. "In Search of a Common Language." *U.S. News and World Report* (27 March): 72.

Lewin, Ralph A., and David K. Jordan. 1981. "The Predominance of English and the Potential Use of Esperanto in Abstracts of Scientific Articles." In *Science and Scientists: Essays by Biochemists, Biologists and Chemists,* edited by M. Kageyama et al., pp. 433–41. Tokyo: Japan Scientific Societies Press.

Lieberman, E. James. 1979. "Esperanto and Trans-National Identity: The Case of Dr. Zamenhof." *International Journal of the Sociology of Language* 20:89–107.

Lins, Ulrich. 1986. *The Contribution of the Universal Esperanto Association to World Peace.* Esperanto Documents 37A. Rotterdam: Universal Esperanto Association.

———. 1988a. *La dangera lingvo.* Gerlingen, Germany: Bleicher.

———. 1988b. *Die gefährliche Sprache.* Gerlingen, Germany: Bleicher.

Lo Jacomo, François. 1981. *Liberté ou autorité dans l'évolution de l'espéranto*. Paris: the author.

McKown, C. J. 1981. *Ses esplorcentroj pri interlingvoj*. Esperanto-Dokumentoj 15E. Rotterdam: Universala Esperanto-Asocio.

Maimon, N. Z. 1978. *La kaŝita vivo de Zamenhof*. Tokyo: Japana Esperanto-Instituto.

Makkink, G. F. 1987. "Pri la artikolo en Esperanto." In *Serta* 1987: 393–405.

Mattos, Geraldo. 1987a. *La deveno de Esperanto*. Chapecó, Brazil: Fonto.

———. 1987b. "Lingvistika priskribo de la verbo en Esperanto." In *Serta* 1987:435–59.

———. 1987c. "Vortanalizo en Esperanto." In Mattos 1987d:169–204.

———. ed. 1987d. *Centjara Esperanto*. Chapecó, Brazil: Fonto.

Maxwell, Dan. 1988. "On the Acquisition of Esperanto." *Studies in Second Language Acquisition* 10:51–61.

Mounin, Georges. 1958. "Pseudo-langues, interlangues et métalangues." *Babel* 4:91–102.

Moya, Giordano. 1989. *Esperanto en prospektivo*. Barcelona: Barcelona Esperanto-Centro.

Neijt, A. 1986. "Esperanto as the Focal Point of Machine Translation." *Multilingua* 5:9–13.

Ockey, Edward. 1982. *A Bibliography of Esperanto Dictionaries/Bibliografio de vortaroj*. Banstead, U.K.: Mondlingvaj Libroj.

Ogden, C. K. 1930. *Basic English*. London: Kegan Paul.

———. 1934. *The System of Basic English*. New York: Harcourt Brace.

Ouyang Wendao and Bruce Sherwood. 1986. *The Language Problem in Science and the Role of the International Language Esperanto*. Esperanto Documents 38A. Rotterdam: Universal Esperanto Association.

Pechan, Alfonso, ed. 1979. *Gvidlibro por supera ekzameno II: Historio, literaturo*. 2d ed. Budapest: Hungara Esperanto-Asocio.

Pei, Mario. 1958. *One Language for the World and How to Achieve It*. Reprint. New York: Biblo and Tannen, 1968.

————. 1965. *Invitation to Linguistics.* New York: Doubleday.

————. 1969. *Wanted: A World Language.* Public Affairs Pamphlet no. 434. New York: Public Affairs Pamphlets.

Pei, Mario, and Frank Gaynor. 1969. *A Dictionary of Linguistics.* Totowa, N.J.: Littlefield Adams.

Pirlot, Germain. 1986. *Oficiala situacio de la Esperanto-instruado en la mondo.* 6th ed. Ostend: the author.

Piron, Claude. 1979. *Understanding among Africans: Linguistic Isolation and Linguistic Communication.* Esperanto Documents 17A. Rotterdam: Universal Esperanto Association. Reprint. Eichholz and Eichholz 1982:282–96.

————. 1981. *Esperanto: European or Asiatic Language?* Esperanto Documents 22A. Rotterdam: Universal Esperanto Association.

————. 1982. "The Psychological Resistance to the International Language." In Eichholz and Eichholz 1982:519–37.

————. 1984. "Contribution à l'étude des apports du yidiche à l'espéranto." *Jewish Language Review* 4:15–29.

————. 1986a. "L'espéranto vu sous l'angle psychopédagogique." *Bildungsforschung und Bildungspraxis/Education et recherche* 8:11–41.

————. 1986b. "Nacieco kaj internacieco de Esperanto." In Umeda 1986: 179–84.

————. 1987a. "Esperanto, formo de humanismo." In *Serta* 1987:571–78.

————. 1987b. *Espéranto: L'image et la réalité.* Saint Denis: Cours et études de linguistique contrastive et appliquée de Vincennes, Université de Paris VIII.

————. 1987c. *L'espéranto, un goût bizarre?* Documents sur l'espéranto 24F. Rotterdam: Association Universelle d'Espéranto.

————. 1988. *Esperanto: Nekonata, miskonata.* Saint Denis: Cours et études de linguistique contrastive et appliquée de Vincennes, Université de Paris VIII.

————. 1989. *La bona lingvo.* Vienna: Pro Esperanto; Budapest: Hungara Esperanto-Asocio.

Piron, Claude, and Humphrey Tonkin. 1979. *Translation in International*

Organizations. Esperanto Documents 20A. Rotterdam: Universal Esperanto Association.

Privat, Edmond. 1930. *Esprimo de sentoj en Esperanto*. 4th ed. The Hague: Internacia Esperanto-Instituto, 1980.

Ragnarsson, Baldur. 1988. *La poezia arto*. Saarbrücken: Artur E. Iltis.

Reiersøl, Olav, and R. C. Marble. 1949. "A Comparison between Word-Formation in Esperanto and English." *Esperantologio* 1:53–58.

Reiersøl, Olav, and Richard E. Wood. 1987. "A Comparison of the Use of Some Suffixes in Esperanto and English." In *Serta* 1987:583–99.

Richardson, David. 1988. *Esperanto: Learning and Using the International Language*. Eastsound, Wa.: Orcas.

Rokicki, Ryszard. 1987. "Leksemstrukturaj aspektoj klasifiki la Esperantan morfemaron." In Duc Goninaz 1987:91–108.

Rossetti, Reto, and Ferenc Szilágyi, ed. 1964. *33 rakontoj: La Esperanta novelarto*. La Laguna, Canary Islands: Stafeto.

Rossetti, Reto, and Henri Vatré, ed. 1990. *Trezoro: Esperanta novelarto 1887–1986*. 2 vols. Budapest: Hungara Esperanto-Asocio.

Rumler, Josef. 1986. *Abunde kaj redunde*. Prague: Ĉeĥa Esperanto-Asocio.

———. 1987. "Koncepto pri la diversaj stiloj kaj ĝia apliko al la Esperanta leksiko." In *Serta* 1987:749–61.

Sadler, Victor. 1991. "Machine Translation Project Reaches Watershed." *LPLP* 15:78–83.

Sadler, Victor, and Ulrich Lins. 1972. "Regardless of Frontiers: A Case Study in Linguistic Persecution." In *Man, Language and Society*, edited by Samir K. Ghosh, pp. 206–15. The Hague and Paris: Mouton.

Saletti, Norberto. 1986. *A History of the World Esperanto Youth Organization*. Esperanto Documents 35A. Rotterdam: Universal Esperanto Association.

Salmon, Vivian G. 1966. "Language Planning in Seventeenth-Century England." In *In Memory of J. R. Firth*, edited by C. A. Bazell et al., pp. 370–97. London: Longman.

———. 1979. *The Study of Language in 17th-Century England*. Amsterdam: Benjamins.

Sapir, Edward. 1961. "The Function of an International Auxiliary Language." In *Culture, Language and Personality*, edited by D. Mandelbaum. Berkeley: University of California Press.

Schleyer, Johann Martin. 1880. *Volapük: Die Weltsprache.* Edited by Reinhard Haupenthal. Hildesheim: Olms, 1982.

Schubert, Klaus. 1987. *Metataxis: Contrastive Dependency Syntax for Machine Translation.* Dordrecht and Providence: Foris.

———. 1988. "Ausdruckskraft und Regelmässigkeit: Was Esperanto für automatische Übersetzung geeignet macht." *LPLP* 12:130–47.

Schubert, Klaus, and Dan Maxwell. 1988. *Interlinguistics: Aspects of the Science of Planned Languages.* Berlin, New York, Amsterdam: Mouton de Gruyter.

Schulz, Richard. 1979. *Europäische Hochsprache oder Sprachimperialismus.* Gerlingen, Germany: Bleicher.

———. 1987. *Sur la vojoj de la Analiza Skolo.* Paderborn, Germany: Esperanto-Centro Paderborn.

Sekelj, Tibor. 1981. *The Language Problem of the Non-Aligned Movement and Its Possible Solution.* Esperanto Documents 26A. Rotterdam: Universal Esperanto Association.

Serta. 1987. *Serta gratulatoria in honorem Juan Régulo.* Vol. 2: Esperantismo. La Laguna, Canary Islands: Universidad de la Laguna.

Shapiro, Barbara J. 1969. *John Wilkins 1614–72: An Intellectual Biography.* Berkeley: University of California Press.

Shenker, Israel. 1987. "Doing Away with All Babble from the Tower of Babel." *Smithsonian* 17:112–25.

Sherwood, Bruce Arne. 1982a. "Statistical Analysis of Conversational Esperanto, with Discussion of the Accusative." *Studies in the Linguistic Sciences* 12:165–82.

———. 1982b. "Variation in Esperanto." *Studies in the Linguistic Sciences* 12:183–96.

———. 1983. *The Educational Value of Esperanto Study: An American View.* Esperanto Documents 31A. Rotterdam: Universal Esperanto Association.

Shumaker, Wayne. 1982. *Renaissance Curiosa.* Binghamton, N.Y.: Medieval and Renaissance Texts.

Slaughter, M. M. 1982. *Universal Languages and Scientific Taxonomy in the Seventeenth Century.* Cambridge: Cambridge University Press.

Spinka, M. 1943. *J. A. Comenius, That Incomparable Moravian.* Chicago: University of Chicago Press.

Staggs, Sam. 1987. "Speaking of Esperanto!" *Frequent Flyer* (May): 63–71.

Stojan, Petr Evstaf'ević. 1929. *Bibliografio de internacia lingvo.* Reprint edited by Reinhard Haupenthal. Hildesheim and New York: Georg Olms, 1973.

Strasser, Gerhard F. 1986. "Seventeenth-Century Catholic Attempts at Revitalizing Latin as a Universal Language." In Tonkin and Johnson-Weiner 1986:55–67.

——. 1988. *Lingua Universalis: Kryptologie und Theorie der Universalsprachen im 16. und 17. Jahrhundert.* Wiesbaden: Otto Harrassowitz.

Symoens, Edward. 1989. *Bibliografio de disertacioj pri Esperanto kaj interlingvistiko/Dissertations sur l'espéranto et l'interlinguistique/Dissertations on Esperanto and Interlinguistics.* Rotterdam: Universala Esperanto-Asocio.

Szerdahelyi, István. 1974. "La karaktero de vortelementoj en Esperanto." *Literatura foiro* 23:8–11; 24:5–9.

——. 1976a. "La semantika modelo de Esperanto." In *Interlingvistika simpozio,* edited by Tišljar, Zlatko, pp. 85–148. Zagreb: Internacia Kultura Servo.

——. 1976b. *Vorto kaj vortelemento en Esperanto.* Kuopio, Finland: Literatura Foiro.

——. 1987. "Principoj de Esperanta etimologio." In Duc Goninaz 1987:109–38.

Thorndike, E. L., et al. 1933. *Language Learning: Summary of a Report.* New York: Bureau of Publications, Teachers College, Columbia University.

Tonkin, Humphrey. 1975. "Poetry in Esperanto: Is an International Literary Culture Possible?" *Proceedings of the Sixth Congress of the International Comparative Literature Association,* pp. 503–7. Stuttgart: Kunst und Wissenschaft.

——. 1977. *Esperanto and International Language Problems: A Research*

Bibliography. 4th ed. Washington, D.C.: Esperantic Studies Foundation.

―――. 1979a. "Equalizing Language." *Journal of Communication* 29: 124–33.

―――. 1979b. *Language and International Communication: The Right to Communicate.* Esperanto Documents 15A. Rotterdam: Universal Esperanto Association. Reprint. *The Right to Communicate: A New Human Right,* edited by Desmond Fisher and L. S. Harms, pp. 185–95. Dublin: Boole, 1983.

―――. 1982. *Esperanto in the Service of the United Nations.* Esperanto Documents 27A. Rotterdam: Universal Esperanto Association.

―――. 1987a. *The International Language Esperanto 1887–1987: Towards the Second Century.* Esperanto Documents 39A. Rotterdam: Universal Esperanto Association.

―――. 1987b. "One Hundred Years of Esperanto: A Survey." *LPLP* 11: 264–82.

Tonkin, Humphrey, Jane Edwards, and W. Verloren van Themaat, ed. 1979–. "Auxiliary Languages. International Languages." *MLA International Bibliography III, Linguistics.* New York: Modern Language Association of America.

Tonkin, Humphrey, and Thomas Hoeksema. 1982. *Esperanto and Literary Translation.* Esperanto Documents 29A. Rotterdam: Universal Esperanto Association.

Tonkin, Humphrey, and Karen Johnson-Weiner, ed. 1986. *The Idea of a Universal Language.* New York: Center for Research and Documentation on World Language Problems.

Tonkin, Humphrey, and Grahame Leon-Smith. 1979. *The Future of Modern Languages in English-Speaking Countries.* Esperanto Documents 18A. Rotterdam: Universal Esperanto Association.

UEA. 1983. *Unesco and the UEA 1976–1982.* Esperanto Documents 32A. Rotterdam: Universal Esperanto Association.

―――. 1991. *Jarlibro 1991.* Rotterdam: Universala Esperanto-Asocio.

Umeda, Yosimi, ed. 1986. *Socilingvistikaj aspektoj de la Internacia Lingvo.* Tokyo: Japana Esperanto-Instituto.

Vatré, Henri. 1986. *Vortstatistikaj esploroj.* Saarbrücken: Artur E. Iltis.

―――. 1987. *Neologisma glosaro.* Saarbrücken: Artur E. Iltis.

Venture, Alec. 1987. "La historio de la Esperantaj lingvaj institucioj." In *Serta* 1987:749–61.

Verax, Charles. 1910. *Enciklopedia vortareto Esperanta*. Paris: Hachette.

Verloren van Themaat, W. A. 1972. "Literature in a Constructed Language." *La Monda Lingvo-Problemo* 4:153–58.

Waringhien, Gaston. 1959. *Lingvo kaj vivo*. La Laguna, Canary Islands: Stafeto.

————. 1970. *Plena ilustrita vortaro de Esperanto*. Paris: Sennacieca Asocio Tutmonda.

Wells, John C. 1978. *Lingvistikaj aspektoj de Esperanto*. Rotterdam: Centro de Esploro kaj Dokumentado pri la Monda Lingvo-Problemo.

Witkam, A. P. M. 1983. *Distributed Language Translation*. Utrecht: BSO.

Wood, Richard E. 1979. "A Voluntary, Non-Territorial Speech Community." In *Sociolinguistic Studies in Language Contact: Methods and Cases*, edited by William Francis Mackey and Jacob Ornstein, pp. 433–50. The Hague: Mouton.

————. 1982. *Current Work in the Linguistics of Esperanto*. Esperanto Documents 28A. Rotterdam: Universal Esperanto Association.

————. 1987. "The Development of Standard Phonology in Esperanto." In Duc Goninaz 1987:40–57.

Zamenhof, Lazar Ludwik. 1903. *Fundamenta krestomatio de la lingvo Esperanto*. 17th ed. Richmansworth, U.K.: Esperanto Publishing Company, 1954.

————. 1905. *Fundamento de Esperanto*. Edited by André Albault. Marmande, France: Editions Françaises d'Espéranto, 1963.

————. 1929. *Originala verkaro*. Edited by J. Dietterle. Leipzig: Ferdinand Hirt.

————. 1948. *Leteroj*. Edited by Gaston Waringhien. 2 vols. Paris: Sennacieca Asocio Tutmonda.

————. 1973–. *Iam kompletigota plena verkaro de L. L. Zamenhof*. Edited by Ludovikito (Itô Kanzi). 14 vols. Osaka: the editor.

Index

A

Academy of Esperanto. *See* Esperanto Academy
Accent in Esperanto, 44, 47–48
Accusative case in Esperanto, 43, 66–68, 72–73, 79, 111
Adam, Eugène (pseud. Lanti), 101, 116
Adamson, Hendrik, 99
Adjectives in Esperanto, 43, 59, 66, 69, 73, 79–80
Adverbs in Esperanto, 44, 62, 67, 69, 73, 79
Affixes in Esperanto, 43, 57–59, 60–61, 64–65, 71, 80, 85–86, 138–39
Agopoff, Noubar, 21
Akademi Internasional de Lingu Universal, 15
Alfandari, Arturo, 21
Allteutonic (Elias Molee), 10
Alphabet of Esperanto, 46
American Philosophical Society, 15
Andersen, Hans Christian, 92, 140
Anglic (R. E. Zachrisson), 11, 21
Antaŭ-Projekto (Jean Effel), 4
Anthologies of national literatures in Esperanto, 93, 107
Anti-Semitism, 25
Apolema (Raoul de la Grasserie), 9, 20

A posteriori languages, 5, 8–12, 19–21; and a priori languages, 6–7
Applebaum, J. D., 104
A priori languages, 5, 7–8, 19–21, 136; and a posteriori languages, 6–7. *See also* philosophical languages
Arabic language, 6, 51, 80
Argus. *See* Ellersiek, Friedrich Wilhelm
Arnim, Wilhelm von, 14–15, 19
Article in Esperanto, 43, 62
Aspect in Esperanto, 57, 70
Atanasov, Atan, 103
Auld, William, xiii, 102, 106, 137, 140, 141
Austin, Manjo, 106
Aymonnier, C., 88

B

Baghy, Gyula (Julio), 95, 99, 104, 106
Balta (Emile Dormoy), 14, 19
Baranovski, Stepan, 4, 19
Baranyai, Emre, 102
Bartelmes, Norbert, 101
Basic English (C. K. Ogden), 11–12, 18, 21
Bauer, Juraj, 14, 19

P